Praise for the show _Dys-Order-Ed_, which ~~~
stories from _Five Fat Sausa~~~_

As a first-time performer at 67, Pam
experience to draw from. With char~
the highs and visceral lows, the fleet~
by disarray and the cruelties of medic   ~~~at willingly
fail to 'see' her ... Within the first half the   ~~~t a dry eye in the house.
We teeter on the brink but are gently reeled back ... Wood emerges
triumphant to reclaim herself, her diagnoses, her sexuality, her
hard-won freedom.

Hannah Francis, _The Age_, Melbourne

It was so wonderful to see the stories I've read in the MS brought
to life by Pam herself! She is exactly as I expected, which clearly
demonstrates how much honesty and true personality come
across in her writing. A truly difficult skill, so very impressive.

Mietta Yans

Praise for the book

She was told she was too much – too big – so she tried to shrink
herself to fit in. But now, FFS is challenging those constraints, carving
out space for herself and anyone else who's ever felt too large. If
you're ready for a ride, step off the merry-go-round and buckle up for
a roller-coaster with Pam. Prepare for a journey full of unpredictable
twists, thrilling highs, and a few detours to ADHDville. Pam's story is
a raw and humorous exploration of her deepest struggles with
mental illness and despair, as well as her exhilarating rise to self-love
and acceptance. With its blend of heartfelt intimacy and sharp wit,
this tale of one woman's battle to live will take you on an emotional
roller-coaster you won't forget. Hold on tight and enjoy the ride.

Mel Kelleher, Clinical Psychologist

FIVE FAT SAUSAGES

First published in 2024 by
Pavlova Press NZ
PO Box 706, Kerikeri
New Zealand
www.pavlovapress.co.nz

Copyright © 2024 Pam Wood
The moral rights of the author have been asserted.
ISBN 978-0-646-70304-6
A catalogue record for this book is available from the National Library of New Zealand.

Cover design by Mietta Yans
Typesetting and internal design by Mietta Yans
Printed on Demand through KDP
Author photo of Pam by Ksenia Belova

**This book contains adult themes, including mention of
childhood sexual abuse, suicide and severe mental health issues.**

FIVE FAT SAUSAGES

PAM WOOD

**Being a roller-coaster
in a merry-go-round world**

Pavlova Press

This book is dedicated to anyone who has struggled with mental health issues or neurodivergence. To anyone who has felt broken, misunderstood or alone, I see you, I acknowledge you. Too many magnificent souls have been lost because their pain has been too big. May you find a source of strength, even if it's just a tiny chink of light, so that despair doesn't engulf you.

Every flower goes through dirt and shit.
Keep blooming your sort of beauty.
A Pammy-ism

The world needs us

I acknowledge the traditional landowners, the
Wurundjeri Woi Wurrung People, of the Kulin Nation.
I have lived on this land for over thirty-seven years.
I pay my respects to the traditional custodians of the
land and extend that respect to Aboriginal elders past,
present, and those yet to come. Thank you for your
care of this land and water for over 40,000 years.
I acknowledge that sovereignty was never ceded.
Always Was, Always Will Be Aboriginal Land.

PART ONE:
How the fuck did I get here?

FFS, writer's block is REAL

FFS, why can't I swear?

FFS, let's start at the real beginning

FFS, don't buy me flowers

FFS, there's a storm brewing

FFS, I'm the smiling depressive!

FFS, here comes the roller-coaster

FFS, that wasn't on the birth plan

FFS, I have ocular toxoplasmosis!

FFS, I'm scared

FFS, I'm back on the toxo wagon

FFS, Pam, don't call it the fat chapter

FFS, I'm FITH

FFS, what's with the money guilt?

FFS, I always assume it's my fault

FFS, it worked!

FFS, Amy Sherman-Palladino, you are NOT my friend

FFS, those were troublesome years

FFS, this is the REAL alcohol chapter

FFS, Kathy Derrick! That wasn't on my list

PART TWO:
Now that I'm here,
what the fuck do I do next?

FFS, who the hell is Bob? (and other sexy disasters)

FFS, I can't fake it till I make it

FFS, there's no such thing as a Mental Health Spa?

FFS, I'm going mad in Madrid

FFS, ask the hard questions

FFS, that's one thing too many

FFS, please insult me, my friend!

FFS, am I anaphylactic to anything positive in my life!!!????

FFS, I CAN do commitment

FFS, procrastination sucks (and it's also expensive)

FFS, my girls are big

FFS, I CAN do something!

FFS, I'm doing a Michelle!

FFS, how can I be getting worse when
I am getting better?

FFS, good luck to you, Leo Dale

Disclaimer

This book contains the truth according to me, Pam Wood,
the Pammy, the daughter, the wife, the mother, the divorcee.
Some people who read this book may not align themselves
with my version of the truth – that is their journey to travel.
This I must accept.

Foreword

Dear Reader

Hello if you know me personally, and welcome if you are a stranger entering my world. The style of this book matches my personality. I speak in an animated way with my whole body and occasionally blurt out random thoughts. This is also how I write.

Most of my story *should* unfold in a way that you'll understand, but we'll go off on tangents and visit seemingly unconnected places. It may become a tad discombobulated and messy – a bit like a roller-coaster's dips and curves. There may come a time when you stop being interested and just want to jump to the end, which you can do, but then you'd miss out on the beauty of the twists and turns.

To start us off, let me tell you about something I learned recently. I had to go to the dentist. Because of childhood dental traumas, I find dental treatment to be panic inducing, so I pre-cried and then called my son on the way there. He repeated my famous and self-regulating words back to me,

'You've got this, Pammy.'

My dentist is lovely, and even with the anxiety I was looking forward to seeing her. I'd broken a bit off my tooth, and she'd told me it would be a straightforward procedure. (End-jumpers, there are no twists with this dental story – no horrible endings about the tooth or the patient.)

As we chit-chatted away, waiting for my face to reach the required nuclear level of numbness, my dentist shared how she was going back to Iran to visit her family for two weeks to introduce her baby to them. I asked when she was going (because I was dreading seeing another dentist if my tooth wasn't magically fixed after this visit), and it was the same day I was planning to leave for a two-week break. We laughed when we realised it would take her less time to get to Iran than it was going to take me to drive the 1100 kilometres to where I was staying.

She asked about my plans for the time away. My answer was, 'To finish the final chapters of my book and review the chapters I've already edited.'

Still waiting for numbness to kick in, she asked me what my book was about. I told her I was writing a memoir about my life so far: the good bits, the bad bits, and some of the wisdom I'd gathered along the way. And how I hoped someone might relate to it and not feel so alone.

She asked me for an example, so I told her about

something that had happened to me as a child – a trauma I'd lived through. After listening to me, she told me she was angry – really, really angry! Even though I assured her I was no longer emotionally attached to the event, she was left in a World of Pain, a World of Shoulds and Should Nots, and was no longer focused on my pending dental procedure. In a nano-second my emotional-trigger-ping-pong trigger got triggered and all my default negative thoughts jumped into my head.

Oh no, I've caused her pain.

I didn't mean to upset her.

I was only trying to give her an example.

She asked, so it's not my fault.

What was I thinking?

My story had affected her in a way I'd never intended. And I started to wonder – if my story could cause pain or distress for someone else, should I actually write it?

Then, in a new and tiny particle of time, I saw the light! All the decades of therapy coalesced into a moment of clarity: *I can't control someone else's reactions.* Other people feel their feelings because they – feel – their – feelings. If my pure intention is to do no harm, they have to take responsibility for their own emotions.

Bing-Bam-Boom. I have no superpowers. All I can do is take responsibility for my own thoughts and actions.

Out of my brain now and back into the reality of the

dentist's chair, a new awareness surfaced – I didn't want an outraged dentist working on my mouth, thank you very much. So I let her talk it out. As I was her last patient for the day, we had the luxury of time. And me being me, after she'd shared some of her own journey around anger, I asked if she would like to do a simple exercise to release some of the pent-up emotion (she hadn't started working on my tooth, remember).

She agreed, and I guided her through a breathing exercise that she said was lovely for her, and which was very reassuring for me. She also told me this was one of the strangest dental appointments she'd ever had. I do tend to have that effect on people!

At the end of the appointment (which went really well for me, by the way), I asked how she was. She said she was still a bit angry. Again, me being me I suggested that at the next session with her therapist she might like to explore why she gets so outraged for others, and boom – there it was, a breakthrough for her. It felt good to have been of some help. Maybe this book won't be so crazy after all.

I gave her a very big hug. She told me something I already knew, that I am a great hugger, and I said, 'Consider yourself Pammed!' Booyah – Dental Therapy with a Twist.

The breakthrough learning for me is that some readers may become triggered. I feel it's my duty to let you know that I am totally okay. I know I live a roller-coaster life, and I've fallen into some massive dips on this metaphorical track, but I have managed to climb out of them. I have dodged, zigzagged, and at times fought for being worthy enough to exist. I am resilient. Maybe a few of you are closing the book slowly now. That's okay. But for those of you willing to carry on, who could resist a blast from the past and a reference to the old *Mission Impossible* shows: *Your mission, Dear Reader, should you choose to accept it, is to read the following chapters knowing that you will not self-destruct.* There might even be opportunities for you to view your own world through different lenses.

And as it says in the tiniest writing on page 947, clause B, Appendix II, the author takes all care and no responsibility. If you're ready to read about life according to Pammy, turn the page.

PS: I cheekily asked for the 'Dental Therapy' rates when I was making payment after my appointment. She grinned and said, 'Definitely next time!'

PART ONE

How the fuck did I get here?

FFS, writer's block is REAL

It's easy – she says.

Just write some words each day – she says.

Surely you can take just sixty seconds to stop and do something routine – she says.

You have already written so much – she says.

When I get in a funk, I just dance it off – she says.

Just write the same word over and over – she says.

I don't dare tell her that these kind and encouraging words merge into blah, blah, blah.

I did try the last strategy once before. I just wrote 'fuck' repeatedly. But all I felt was a familiar despair: here was yet another thing I couldn't motivate myself to do.

I also pondered how many times I could write this fabulously expressive word before I got bored and some sort of creativity urged me to write something more meaningful. Maybe it would work if I wrote it 19,370 times. Yes, that would be an excellent procrastination strategy.

Recently in a coaching chat (that I wanted to avoid as I hadn't written anything for weeks and I'd run out of marginally valid excuses), I was asked, 'What's going on?'

I didn't use the words 'writer's block' because I don't consider myself a writer yet (and the way I'm going I'll successfully achieve 'not being a writer') but instead fessed up to filling my days with so many other things. The irony that I was living in one of the longest Covid lockdowns in the history of the universe – on my own with basically nothing to fill my days – did not occur to me at that moment.

I had so many reasons, excuses, blah blah blahs and finally fell back on the old, handy, cringeworthy explanation that I am just disorganised. None of my good intentions ever seemed to translate to actions. The truth was that I'd written many chapters in my head (some of which I considered exceptional in my muddled moments of self-aggrandisement); however, I didn't make the time to even try to write anything. My PhD in Procrastination was surely in the post.

My ever-helpful coach suggested that perhaps, just maybe, I could try a regular, simple activity. I sat in a state of fear, wondering what she was going to propose. She suggested that I set my phone timer for sixty seconds and just sit and watch it count down to zero at least once a day. BOOM – my brain erupted like Vesuvius.

While I sat calmly on the Zoom meeting, looking as though

I was considering this very basic task, my brain was exploding with screaming thoughts, all competing for that micro-nanosecond they desperately needed. Thoughts and questions such as:

* What are you so scared about? This is such a simple request.

* Why can't I just say yes and move on from this horrible and uncomfortable feeling?

* Because then I would have to try to do it, and what if I can't do it? What if I fail? How can I fail at such a simple task?

* Why are you so pathetic that you cannot even find sixty seconds a day that you can commit to?

* Give up - you will never be a writer. You can't even watch sixty seconds disappear. Everyone will know you are a fraud.

* Why can't I commit to anything? Fuck, she's still looking at me! What do I say now?

* Oh no - she's still there, sitting and waiting for me to reply. She's just wanting to be helpful. You bloody paid her to be helpful. Look, she's so keen to help you. SAY SOMETHING!

So, I said, 'I can't tell you right now why this seems so hard to commit to.'

And then she said something like, 'You can do it. Can you promise to do it?'

NOOOOOOO – she used the word 'PROMISE'!

Back to the screaming fireworks in my brain that would make the Sydney Harbour New Year's Eve display pale into insignificance.

* She wants me to promise! But what happens if I can't do it? Oh, please, don't make me lie to her when she really is just wanting to help me. She is so nice; I don't want to lie to her. But how can I PROMISE to do it when I'm not sure if I really can?

* You are so pathetic. It is one minute. Sixty seconds. She's now suggesting strategies about how to accomplish it. WHAT?

* Such a simple task - why can't you even commit to this one simple task?

A few seconds passed and she must have seen the rising panic – or maybe my internal vomiting at my own uselessness was somehow visible in my deer-in-headlights eyes – and she said, 'Maybe this is something you could consider and see if it is helpful.'

The last firework faded, leaving only a hint of smoke.

Our coaching call concluded with a discussion of how I find regular commitments paralysing and how the 'exploding fireworks brain' syndrome probably needs some further exploration.

Days and days passed.

They were mostly spent in bed.

I didn't want to get up because that might mean I'd have to face the fact I can't even commit to watching a clock tick down for sixty seconds. Getting out of bed might mean I'd be tasked with doing other simple things around the house, like a bit of tidying or putting clean clothes away. It all became overwhelming, so I went to the toilet, grabbed a few dry biscuits, cut up a bit of cheese to be gourmet and went back to bed.

My bed is like a cocoon. I can hide in there. I can ignore the phone. I can ignore the doorbell. If my body complies and I sleep, I don't have to be aware of all of the things that I'm not doing, that I am not achieving, all the things that I'm pretending don't matter. And then, 'Well, no one cares anyway!'

When darkness fell I crept out of bed like a bloodless, dehydrated, retired vampire, knowing I was safe now. The day was done. I'd survived and managed to hide my patheticness. I stayed up very late in the hope I'd be so tired when I finally crashed that I wouldn't wake up until late afternoon.

This whole way of thinking seems so alien to others. They try to tell me about how wonderful I am, how I've changed lives – but there always is a big BUT.

BUT, says the Inner Critic, if you really knew me you wouldn't be saying these lovely things. If you only knew how I waste my days, how I hide from the world, how unproductive I really am, how I can't even do the basic things, then you wouldn't think I was so talented, so kind, so wise.

In my experience, the seriously shit thing about depression is that it is like a creeping amoeba. It slowly starts a journey towards you, and then it does what an amoeba does – it begins to engulf your brain, like a positive-thought-seeking engulfer. It insidiously smothers your joy, your self-worth and any moment of pleasure until you are powerless. And this blob, with its heavy weight of dark thoughts, eliminates any light.

After more therapy than all of the *Real Housewives of Beverley Hills* put together, I can finally recognise one or two patterns that might be indicators of my impending poor mental health cycle.

Usually, after having hidden from the world for more than a few days, I start to write the most apologetic text or email to one or two particular people – the ones who I know love me dearly. I tell them they deserve a better version of me, that their lives would have been so much better if I wasn't their mother or their friend, and that I'll take ownership for every time I have disappointed them or let them down ... vomit, vomit, vomit.

This time I'd started to write the same version of my self-loathing when all those years of therapy sparked a thought: *Pammy, maybe you shouldn't have cancelled that appointment with the psychiatrist yesterday. Oh, you sausage, you little fat sausage, ring and ask for a call-back – you are struggling, my dear!*

I deleted the self-effacing text and replaced it with one saying, 'I am doing it tough.' I made the call to my psychiatrist and then got back in touch with the world.

Challenging the Inner Critic (also known as that creepy little shitty amoeba brain of despair) is tough. HAHAHA – tough is such an understatement! It feels like I'm climbing Mt Everest walking backwards dragging forty-two elephants (and their trainers), and all the while believing I should be able to do it, so why can't I do it? Until a trusted therapist or understanding friend says, 'It's not Mt Everest, Pammy. It's a nasty pimple turned to pus and the elephants don't even want to go anywhere near it, so let them go! And then pop that sucker.' (Too much? Maybe it is a bit too much. I thought I was going so well with the metaphor. Oh, well – the editor will probably take it out anyway!)

I truly wish I could see the amoeba way earlier and step out of its way. Or say, 'Hello, amoeba – sorry, I'm not receiving guests right now.'

And then, with a little help from my friends (how I love you, Joe Cocker – The Beatles never really did the song justice), I get to see that the conversation about the sixty seconds was not the trigger. The trigger that let the amoeba out of the gate (I like this analogy – the little shape-shifting amoeba is actually quite cute) was really something else completely.

It was about commitment. I got that bit right. But I had to confront something way larger than making a commitment (promise) to watch a timer count down for sixty seconds. I was confronted by having to make a commitment to potentially changing the direction of my life.

Enter dramatic music – dun da da daaaaaahhhh darrrrr. Stay tuned! Same Bat Place, Same Bat Channel. (I am seriously old!)

My biggest fear is that my neediness will distance us and you will think that I am just too hard work to be around. And/or that you will feel obligated to spend time with me.

FFS, why can't I swear?

Apparently, the beginning is a very good place to start, at least according to writing rules and Julie Andrews in her glorious rendition of the musical alphabet. Thanks, Julie – great advice.

BUT I am a creative, and I find structure incredibly limiting. Why should I have to start at the very beginning? Maybe I'll just start in the middle. It might end up looking a tad all over the place, and a bit chaotic to those who like a little or a whole lot of Julie Andrews' philosophy, but I think it's a good place to start.

The middle of my story occurred in my mid-to-late thirties when the Five Fat Sausages concept was conceived.

My friend Lyn is part of a family we affectionately called The Swearing Burkes. I can publicly name them as they all embrace this title. Whenever we used to visit The Swearing Burkes, I would tell my children to put invisible swear filters on their ears so the swear words wouldn't enter their brains. Of course, this didn't work, and my kids adored these visits.

One day Lyn and I had one of our very long phone calls.

On this call I felt safe enough to share my shameful secret – I was suffering from acute and chronic depression and was on a large amount of antidepressants. I felt so ashamed that I couldn't cope; the stupid antidepressants weren't working; I was always letting people down; I thought I was crazy; I wasn't a good mother – and so it went on.

Lyn's response was (swearing alert), 'For fuck's sake! I can't believe it.'

(Dear Reader, perhaps I should have offered a swearing alert earlier, but from now on there will be no more swearing alerts. If you feel the need, please grab your swear-filter glasses now.)

As the conversation continued and I shared more and more, her response continued to be *FFS* in disbelief, over and over again. We laughed. I cried. She swore lots. She said positive thing after positive thing about me, but I was like Teflon – it all slid right off.

By the end of the call I'd come to two realisations: I could absolutely accept that I was kind ... and I couldn't swear! Even with her enthusiastic encouragement, I still felt bound to be the good girl. (Oh, how the tides have turned.)

Then it occurred to me that instead of using Lyn's words, I could easily say 'five fat sausages' (from the childhood song) when I was frustrated or whenever things seemed out of control. These became my secret swear words, and every time I said them out loud I had a silent giggle. (Yep – my tumultuous ride along my crazy roller-coaster track all of a sudden seemed more manageable.)

Sometimes I would say 'five very, very, very fat sausages'. Sometimes I would sing, 'five fat fat fat sausages' to a made-up tune. Feeling bold enough to say 'five fat sausages', and knowing it was Lyn's and my private joke, caused me moments of joy in some very dark, lonely and stressful motherhood moments. I tried hard never to say it in anger so others wouldn't find out my secret and take away my inner joy.

My family eventually worked it out, the good girl returned and the inner glee died. Except for private chats with Lyn, it took eons before I could use the real words.

Over the years I have shared my Five Fat Sausages story with young mums and know that my once inner glee now continues in the hearts of others.

My roller-coaster life has been thrilling at times, unpredictable and fun. And sometimes very scary. So scary that I couldn't tell anyone except for a select few about the dips, hoping my roller-coaster would turn a corner and I'd start to climb again. I knew exactly how it felt when I was about to fly off the tracks. The reality of a crash and burn was not pretty. I didn't know any other roller-coaster people – at least, none who would admit to it – and I was married to a very stable merry-go-round man who seemed so normal.

I was a total failure at conforming to this socially acceptable merry-go-round way of life. Others seemed to do it so easily. Little ups, little downs. A life of predictability. A this-too-shall-pass type of ride. I was so ashamed that my multiple medications and I couldn't control my roller-coaster. I lived in fear of people finding out about my mental illness, terrified they would judge me harshly. Who would trust me as an organisational change consultant? How could anyone love me, or even like me? And my very worst fear – that I was defective, and that this would be discovered by all!

Thirty-plus years post my Five Fat Sausage discovery, I can now say the real words: 'For Fuck's Sake, if you've got it, own it, and I'm going to be the best fucking roller-coaster I can be.'

And you know what, Dear Reader? I now realise I'm not the only roller-coaster in a merry-go-round world. Maybe you're one too.

Although I have always wanted to be perfect in many areas of my life, I can't be. I will make mistakes. Sometimes I will make the same mistakes thinking that if it is said or done in a different way it might work! Whoever originally said 'Insanity is doing the same thing over and over and expecting different results' seems to be correct, from my experience.

FFS, let's start at the real beginning

Okay, Julie, you may have been a superstar in your day but fuck, I hate it when you're right. I give in, I'll do the acceptable thing and start at the very beginning. If my life were a fairy tale, this is how it could have been written:

Once upon a time, a baby girl called Pamela Joy Wood entered this Big, Wide World. She was born on 31 October 1956, Halloween night, in the witching hour between eleven o'clock and midnight. She was the second girl, and by all accounts a very good girl – until she wasn't.

Let's look back at times gone past, way before PJW was a twinkling in either of her parents' eyes.

The future mother of Pamela Joy Wood, Ruth Ann Billett, was born in 1924. She was her mother's eldest child but her father's third. His first wife had died, and he had two daughters from this previous marriage.

Ruth's mother was strict, demanding and intimidating. Little Ruth was trained to be seen and not heard, and she lived in fear of making anyone angry. These qualities shaped her whole life.

Ruth's father was a larrikin. He worked on the docks, was an early unionist and communist and slipped around the edges of the law. He was a bit of a lad and a big drinker, but he was the one that provided the small windows of joy Ruth had in her early years.

A few years after Ruth was born, the boy child arrived. He was the apple of his mother's eye and could do no wrong. Little Ruth grew to know she would never be his equal and that her dreams of becoming a maths teacher were impossible; the boy child was destined to become the educated one.

Ruth grew up to be a serious, quiet, shy, socially awkward and unworldly girl. She was a homebody, protected and dominated by her mother. She began work in the austere and serious world that existed in the final stages of WW2, compliantly taking on appropriate jobs and waiting to get married.

While Ruth was taking her first steps into adulthood, her future husband, Jack, was fighting for his life as a commando in New Guinea as part of the Australian Army.

Jack was the youngest of seven children born to parents who were cold and hard to please. He grew up in Tasmania during the Great Depression, barely finished primary school, and was taught to hustle to make money any way he could. At sixteen he asked his mother to illegally sign his enlistment papers and escaped his miserable life to join the Australian

Army. It all sounded like a fabulous adventure – be with the blokes, get fed three times a day, get paid, kill the enemy and defend Australia. He finally had a purpose in life.

Jack knew what hard work was like, he knew how to be sneaky, and he loved the other men who took this young bloke under their wings. He could laugh, joke and be free from the burden of his harsh life back in Tassie. He had total disrespect for authority and was involved in – and often instigated – numerous pranks. He accepted whatever punishment came his way; the fun seemed worth it, and he still got fed.

After his basic training he decided to train as a commando – a soldier highly skilled in stealth and hand-to-hand combat. Their job in WW2 was to sneak up on the enemy and kill them as quickly and quietly as possible, paving an easier path for the other soldiers to come in behind them. While in New Guinea on the Kokoda Track, my father killed many Japanese soldiers. He learnt to lie still for hours and listen for a twig to snap. He lay in mud-filled trenches in torrential rain and witnessed his true mates – his commando family – being killed under horrendous circumstances. He was the only survivor of his small team but had no time to grieve before he was placed with another unit of surviving commandos.

Hours upon hours in the muddy trenches and hastily built shelters riddled his body with dysentery and tapeworms. By the end stages of the war he was as weak as a kitten and around 1945 was transported back to Darwin to be hospitalised.

Once he'd recovered his strength he didn't go back to his hometown, Launceston. He had nothing to go back to. He headed to Melbourne, and the very first thing he did when he got there was to burn his uniform and his dreaded paybook that recorded every misdemeanour he'd ever committed during his time of service. How he spent his time between then and when he met Ruth in 1950 is a mystery.

They met at GJ Coles – he was a storeman and she was in administration. She was perfect wife material. Their courtship involved meeting every Friday night at her house and playing cards together with her parents. He was her first boyfriend. After a year of courtship they got engaged. They may have kissed a few times and then they got married.

Their wedding night set the standard for their entire relationship. Unlike Jack, who had great sexual adventures in his training days and during R&R in the war, Ruth was a virgin. She had absolutely no sexual experience nor any idea of what to expect. Ruthie told me later that her very first negligee had been made by her mum, created from recycled nylon given to my nanna by one of Mum's married stepsisters for Ruth's wedding night. And she'd told Ruth to be grateful that someone wanted her.

On that first night as husband and wife, Jack had drunk a skinful of beer and Ruth hadn't had one drop – she was a good girl. When the inevitable consummation approached Ruth was clueless. Jack told her he hadn't thought she'd be so frigid, and subsequently 'took her'.

This was the start of their marriage. They lived unhappily ever after. The End.

When my brain thinks I'm being threatened, potentially isolated or that I don't belong, my actions will be based solely on my emotions and any perceived imminent threat.

In these times I will probably take actions that may not be best in the long term for myself or others. Therefore, before this happens, I need to somehow extricate myself from the threat.

FFS, don't buy me flowers

As I write this, it's coming up to my birthday and I am being honest with all my friends with this reminder – please do not buy me flowers. EVER. I know some people like to buy flowers for a special occasion, but I am outing myself. The only flowers I value are the ones picked from someone's garden. For my birthday I do like to be celebrated with a kind thought, a big hug or a long phone call, reminding me I am loved. And I also love a good card! Hint, hint!

I know I have some sort of PTSD around bought flowers. It started during my childhood. Every Mother's Day, for her birthday and often just before Christmas, my mum used to receive a big box of delivered flowers. She always seemed surprised and delighted when they arrived, profusely thanking our dad and making a big display of reading out the card: *Dear Ruth, Happy [insert occasion here]. Love Jack.* When Dad stopped pretending he had anything to do with them, I realised Mum was ordering them for herself.

The flowers were placed in full view on the top of the

refrigerator. We had no visitors and no one to show them off to, but there they stayed. To my knowledge, they were never watered or attended to. They slowly lost their lustre and their ability to stand tall. They wilted and bent over. Defeated, they shrivelled up and died a sad and lonely death. When I was old enough to reach the top of the fridge, it became my job to take the dead flowers down. I had to remove the slimy, smelly stems from the green shit the flowers were stuck into, throw them out and put the green shit in the cupboard just in case Mum wanted to use it again. She never did.

I used to save the ribbons that came with the flowers, thinking I might use them one day. I so wanted to have long hair, to put a ribbon in it, to have something pretty, but I had no say in things like this. My hair was always kept short as this was practical. I ended up having a huge collection of useless, pretty frippery that I gave up on long before I was a teen.

This charade was repeated year after year after year and I came to dread the arrival of dead flowers waiting to happen. Eventually, Mum got smarter and started buying things she wanted for herself, including brooches, clothing, and once even an iron. She'd buy them, wrap them and open them with great delight on her birthday or Christmas Day, always thanking my father for the gift.

To give you an idea of how deeply the flower charade affected me, I need to tell you about my wedding day. It is such a long 'can only happen to Pammy' story that it deserves a whole book, but I'll try to give you the summarised version.

I didn't want anything to die on my wedding day, especially flowers, so I decided to wear dried flowers in my hair and to carry a bouquet of dried flowers. I even made my own place cards with little sprigs of dried flowers attached. 'Ohhh, how sweet!' I hear you croon.

No flowers died that day, but one of my father-in-law's best friends dropped dead during the last dance! My friend, a nurse, started cardiac compressions, and as I had ski patrol first aid training I did mouth to mouth. When we got tired the boys took over – the newly wedded man and his PE-trained buddy. They worked on Mr B until the ambulance came.

In shock, we cancelled the after party and cried together for two days on our honeymoon before returning home early from our planned fortnight away. But neither of us had really wanted to be there anyway, and consummating the marriage was not going to happen anytime soon!

The first people we saw afterwards were our friends who later in our married life we named the Swearing Burkes.

I lamented that I hadn't wanted anything to die on my wedding day, but look what had happened.

Lyn didn't mince words. 'For fuck's sake, what were you thinking? Your flowers were already DEAD.'

Her words were a balm that forever cemented our

friendship and love of dark humour. We laughed and laughed and laughed about it for years.

Later in our marriage my husband became a spontaneous flower giver. He was a keen vegetable gardener but took no interest in growing flowers, so he would purchase them for me. Of course I accepted them graciously. Any reasons for not wanting them seemed silly – and besides, I'd buried my past so deeply, how could bought flowers possibly affect me now?

But as our marriage declined and our finances increased he began to buy them for me every Saturday after his morning swim. He thought he was being a good husband, but he never asked whether I liked him buying flowers for me or not. And I didn't have the voice or the courage to share my dread of knowing I would be the person reliving my childhood distress week after week

They were just more dead flowers waiting to happen. Even though I took good care of them and tried to keep them alive, they eventually drooped, dropped petals and pollen, and ultimately died. Each week I was back in my past with slimy stalks, smelly water and a filthy vase that needed cleaning. Death happened around the Thursday, and I knew by Saturday there would be more flowers for me to deal with.

Lilies were the worst. He loved them, I hated them – but I never told him. I knew he wouldn't understand that I associated them with death. I still lived in fear of being a disappointment to him. If I appeared ungrateful, would I then receive the silent treatment that was my father's instrument of torture? So I tolerated the resentment and then the resignation – this was my lot in life and I had to make it work somehow. I felt I was beyond help anyway.

Since my earlier demand – *Please do not buy me flowers, ever!* – I have realised I need to confess that I do love flowers. I love looking at them in gardens and I am a 'sniff any sort of rose' person, hoping that it will have a beautiful scent.

I also love it if someone cares enough to pick flowers out of their garden for me. My father-in-law, a lovely, kind man, delighted in gifting people bunches of flowers from his huge garden, and I loved receiving those flowers grown with love.

When my mum died and we had to sell her house, I tried to transplant some of her beloved roses to my new post-divorce house. Some of them were over forty years old. They didn't transplant well and all except one died during the first year. The one that survived was Just Joey, my mum's favourite. It has a divine scent – in contrast to bought flowers, which usually smell of nothing except the money spent.

After the first year, Ruthie Rose – my new name for Just Joey – had a knobbly trunk with one living branch that produced one flower. I was so excited, I felt like I had created life again. When I sniffed it I felt my mum smiling, so proud that her rose could give me some joy. I took photos of this single, glorious, apricot flower and sent them to my sister, who was my partner in crime in the initial theft of the plants. Year upon year my Ruthie Rose continues to delight me with about twenty flowers that arrive in groups of two or three, and my joy escalates with each sniffing. Sometimes I cut a few flowers to bring a bit of my past inside.

Beliefs formed in childhood are like a
pair of unconscious glasses that impact
how we see the world. I viewed the world
in shoulds – I should be this, I should
not be that, others should or shouldn't
be something else. These glasses
progressively became thicker and
thicker with each of my perceived flaws.

FFS, there's a storm brewing

As a child, I thought my father loved thunder and lightning. Whenever there was a storm he would wake me up and we'd go out onto the verandah. Dad would sit on an old metal chair with his two best mates beside him – his favourite dog on one side and his long-necked bottle of beer on the other. I sat on a little stool next to him on the dog's side because there would be 'hell to pay if anyone knocks over my beer'.

I have fond memories of sitting out with my dad, in my pyjamas, watching for a storm to come. If it was a bit cold Dad would let me wear his dressing gown, a big, brown, chequered, pure-wool thing that smelt of body odour – not overwhelming but quite strong and always present.

Every now and then small flashes would light up part of the sky. The crickets kept singing while we waited for the rumble of thunder. A dog, or Dad, might sigh, snort or fart, and when the thunder finally came Dad would say, 'That's still a long way away. Don't start counting yet.'

I remember gibbering excitedly, since spending time alone

with Dad was something very rare. He didn't talk much and seemed to tolerate my noise. Every now and then he'd lean sideways to pick up the longneck and fill his glass to the tippy-top. I never knew why he would pour this beer so carefully into a slightly angled glass and then turn it up straight at the end. It looked like it had ice-cream on top, and when he took the first sip of his new glassful he always gave a gentle sigh.

As we sat, the lightning would flash and the thunder would get a tiny bit louder each time. We'd both stare expectantly into the sky. Sometimes it looked like God had briefly turned on a lamp in a cloud and then flicked it off again. 'If the next one is louder, we'll start counting,' Dad would say.

The next time the lightning flashed I'd get so excited and Dad would start the countdown: 'One – cat and dog; two – cat and dog ...' until we heard the thunder. After the first countdown I'd wait with great anticipation for the next one. I wanted to see great bolts of lightning and hear the thunder boom really loud.

A flash, even brighter! Whoo-hoo! We would start the count out loud together: 'One – cat and dog ...' As the storm grew closer and the thunder louder, the world became silent in those moments between the claps – it was just my dad and me. When I was quite young, if the counting stopped at two I'd be sent inside to watch from the lounge window. The dogs would already have beaten a hasty retreat to a hiding place and I was alone peeking out. The sky would light up and

I would count 'One – cat and dog' until I heard the crack of thunder – *BOOM*. I was scared but whenever I looked out at my dad he was sitting there passively with his beer. As I grew older I was allowed to sit out there with him, saying less each time.

There were two occasions when the thunder and lightning came at the same time. The noise was unimaginable – like a small bomb. The house and my body shook and the sound stayed ringing in my ears. The dogs had hidden themselves inside and we could hear them whimpering. Dad reached over and squeezed my shoulder tightly – there were no words. He kept hold just in case there was another bone-shaking roar. Torrential rain followed and it seemed as if the thunder and lightning had broken the dams of heaven. At some stage I went to bed, leaving him sitting there – a silhouette pouring another glass of beer with an ice-cream topping.

I thought Dad loved thunder and lightning too, but looking back at those moments, and now knowing my dad probably had serious, unaddressed wartime PTSD, I don't know that he did love them. During our years of storm watching, I'd learned that he and his army mates could work out whether a storm was coming towards them or going away. And that, when lying in the ditches waiting to attack or retreat, thunderstorms could give them an opportunity for cover. So, did he love storms? Or did he just want to be outside so he knew where the loud noises were coming from, rather than being caught unawares and woken by a loud, unexpected, house-rattling BOOM?

And what a bonus – his youngest child wanted to hang out with him and the dogs in the late hours of the night. And maybe this helped him keep his demons at bay.

Beyond this, Dad rarely spoke of his time in the war. I knew it must have been horrible because every Anzac Day and Remembrance Day he would disappear, usually to the local RSL, or into himself out the back with his beer and his dogs. These disappearances mostly lasted a day or so, but sometimes it was much longer than that. We were never told why. We were just told to be careful if Dad was around on those days.

I knew my dad didn't believe in God, but it was during our thunderstorm watching that he shared with me two of his beautiful theories of life.

His first theory went like this: *If there is a God, thunderstorms are His way of getting people's attention. He was going to send lots of rain to wash the world clean again and give all the plants, and us, a chance to grow.* How lovely for a little girl to live in hope that love could grow for her. It set her up to think that forgiveness was possible and that people and circumstances could always change for the better.

The other theory Dad shared with me was that, *If there is a God, He's made up of all the smiles in the world and it's our duty to keep smiles alive and make others smile because that makes for a powerful God and a better world.* Beautiful theory – except Dad rarely smiled. He always seemed annoyed or wanted to be on his own. On reflection, this one seriously fucked me up! It built a belief system where I felt responsible for making people smile. I was responsible for their happiness. And if I couldn't make others smile, no one, including God, would ever be happy with me.

It's incredibly sad that my dad didn't apply any of these principles to his own life yet they defined me. In spite of all that, I still get excited about thunderstorms and the thought that everything is being washed away to start anew.

Without my own thunderstorms I would not be the person I am today. A person who most of the time owns her mental health journey, has two beautiful children who are blessings in their own way to the world, has great compassion for others, and forgives her parents, understanding that they would have never willingly wanted to hurt or damage her in any way.

FFS, I'm the smiling depressive!

The smiling depressive? What an oxymoron! How can someone be smiling when they have depression? Well, I am proof this is possible. I still manage to smile even though my current diagnosis is acute and chronic major depressive disorder, complex childhood PTSD, high-functioning ADHD, acute maladaptive beliefs about self-worth, and being hypercritical of self with unrelenting personal standards.

Wow, what a fun person to be around! Thankfully, after loads of therapy, I learned that some aspects of mental health can be inherited. Dear Reader, while I don't go into the genetic links behind mental health in this book, I can't tell you how relieved I was to hear that my complexities might not be all my fault.

That is the nature part; the other avenue is through the nurture route. Most formative beliefs are established in childhood – a time when, in theory, a person develops feelings of safety and self-worth and a platform on which to build healthy relationships.

Growing up with complex childhood issues and parents who were, themselves, only just surviving, a little girl … a teenager … an adult started to believe certain things about herself.

Fuck Fuck Fuck Fuck – I tried to write another 4500 fucks to fill in the page so I wouldn't have to tell the story, but it didn't work.

My mum was brought up to be a good girl, to be seen and not heard, and she based her own parenting beliefs on this. My sister and I *had* to be good. This was partly so Mum could be at her most efficient in the whirlwind of household chores she created after work and on the weekends. (Our family could never count on a regular income from Dad, so Mum was the breadwinner as well as the housewife.) But it was also because Dad could easily be triggered into a lengthy period of silence and drinking, and a morosity that seemed to suck the energy from anyone in close proximity. The words *Don't upset your dad* are burned into my brain.

Early in my childhood Dad encouraged the cheekiness in me and we had a few laughs, but he never seemed to be there to defend me when I got in trouble. I don't believe I brought many smiles to my mum.

I can't remember how old I was when Dad told me his smile theory. Maybe nine or ten. Of course, Dad didn't live by this principle at home. I can barely remember him and Mum sharing a smile or a laugh except when – rarely – there were other people at our house. When Dad was with others he was always joking around and making people laugh. He seemed so well liked. In my child's brain, it's likely I combined my mother's demands that I be a good girl with my dad's instructions to make other people smile to make God happy. What a burden. I tried so hard to make people smile, though by the time I was about twelve I gave up on making my mum smile. And by then Dad was an unpredictable entity. In all my teen memories we were tippy-toeing around him, so bringing a smile to his face seemed very difficult.

Inside I was a desperate child, craving to be loved. Negative attention was better than no attention, so I received many smacks and the occasional beating. I knew I'd crossed the line when Mum started dropping me off at Sunday School. She wasn't particularly religious, and neither of her children was christened, so this was a form of punishment, administered in the hope I'd learn to be a better girl. I knew I was bad and needed to be fixed, and since Mum had given up on me, God had to do it.

Seriously, WTF were you thinking, Ruthie? Looking back, it's no surprise this wasn't effective. If I saw someone outside the church and they smiled at me I might go in, but most of the time I'd hide around the back until people were coming out. Then I knew it was time for me to start walking home on my own.

I got really good at the 'God Game', even if I do say so myself. After a while I started to tell Mum how much I liked going to Sunday School. I told her I had great fun there – well, I did have fun out the back looking for snails and lizards – so when I was about to be punished I'd beg to be allowed to keep going to Sunday School even though I had been *so* naughty. My punishable misdemeanours at this stage might have been making a mess in the bathroom and not cleaning it up properly, or hiding when Mum was calling me to help her wash the dishes. When Mum announced that my punishment would be to miss Sunday School that week I thought I was very clever! The whole concept of God saving me seemed to have slipped off the agenda.

But the scars of being responsible for other people's happiness, and of being a good girl, lingered in my soul. I believed even God had given up on me, and the only way I could be accepted was to make others smile so they'd like me. The need to hide the bad part of me began early in my life.

This lack of self-worth and the burden of knowing I should never upset other people was heavy and may have been what led to the emergence of the Smiling Depressive. In my early teens I would defiantly suffer the consequences of Mum's physical punishments, which escalated over time, and equally the serious consequences of psychological punishment from Dad that triggered a never-ending quest for feelings of love and belonging.

For me, there are a number of 'if onlys' in Dad's theories and Mum's expectations: if only Dad's first thunderstorm theory of life had included a *Get Out of Jail Free* card so I could believe I'd be forgiven, and even loved, despite God needing to wash me every now and again; if only I could have believed a fresh start was possible and hadn't felt doomed to be the naughty one – that would have been so liberating; if only Dad and Mum could smile, and if only I could have smiled from joy rather than as a duty to make other people happy. If only I'd been allowed to be angry, to be sad, to have a thunderstorm of emotions, to feel comforted, to feel accepted as I was and to not have to be a good girl.

Fuckity fuck I'm tired now!

Sometimes I long for a merry-go-round
life, but I have to admit – at least the
roller-coaster lets me experience
life full on.

FFS, here comes the roller-coaster

My mother was always in a hurry to get things done. She was the man of the house and often worked three jobs at a time. She'd leave home at 7am and get back just in time for dinner. It seemed to me that she was the only mother who had to work. All my friends' mothers were home at the end of the school day and turned up to parent–teacher conferences.

Mum was incredibly shy and, on reflection, had few social skills compared to Dad. She had a need to control our lives, had great expectations as to what we should or shouldn't be doing, and was quick with a corrective smack (or several).

She was always in a hurry to get us into bed and out of her hair. She had no friends that I knew of and never seemed happy. She spent her life working, either at her paid jobs or at home, and was ever vigilant that we didn't upset Dad. This was probably because she'd be included in the dead-to-me silence Dad partook of until he decided he'd punished us enough for upsetting him.

Kudos must go to Dad in one way. I was never smacked by him. Although sometimes I wish I had been. It would have been quick, and maybe we could've moved on. Nope – Dad's preferred method of punishment was those long periods of emotional withdrawal. I knew when it was my fault, but there were times when none of us understood who was to blame.

I have no memory of ever being read to, hugged, or feeling close to Mum. My belief that she didn't love me was reinforced when I was about eight years old and I asked her not to leave me at home with Pop, my dad's father, any more. I pointed to my private parts and told her Pop had been touching me and doing things down there and I didn't like it. I also didn't like having to kiss him because he smelt and he stuck in his tongue. Mum instantly smacked me, told me not to be such a bad girl and not to tell tales. It wasn't until four decades later that we finally spoke about it.

I continued to receive lots of evidence that I was too much or not enough, and just like some dormant virus, Dear Reader, variations of these thoughts still arise.

Dad was occasionally fun, but he was also silent and dismissive. His best loves were Victoria Bitter and whatever dogs we had at the time. He spent his day trying to fob off stolen goods and most nights either getting drunk at the RSL or drinking outside with the dogs, listening to the radio playing quietly in the background. Sometimes he didn't come home for days, and when he was at home we never knew which dad it would be. I always hoped it would be the happy dad, but those times got further and further apart.

During our early primary school years Dad would come home around five o'clock, always smelling of beer, and would turn on the vegetables my sister and I had prepared. If Mum hadn't made a stew the night before, he'd turn on the grill to cook whatever meat had been left out to thaw. We knew early on that Dad would never touch raw meat, so we had to put it on the cold grill before he got home. How we never got food poisoning amazes me. Maybe the fact that my mum overcooked everything was the reason.

By the time I was in my last years of primary school, Dad no longer came home until he wanted to. We knew he was at the RSL (I never knew what that meant but I knew it was a bad place) and his dinner would be put on a plate to slowly steam to death, for him to eat (if he was drunk enough) when he got home.

Mum and Dad's relationship deteriorated as Dad slowly disappeared into anger and righteousness and Mum into co-dependence, enabling his rude and demeaning behaviour. By the time I finished high school, I had no respect for and no relationship with either of them.

Having parents who couldn't provide a safe and nurturing environment created a stage for my eternal quest for love and validation. Luckily (hahaha) I was born to challenge and grow beyond my circumstances. If only I'd had a Mary Poppins to be my guide (Julie – where were you when I needed you?) I might have been less self-destructive.

In terms of sexuality, what a mess that was. I have no memory of noticing any difference between boys and girls before I was thirteen. I was a competitive swimmer, and in those days (when dinosaurs roamed the Earth) boys and girls trained together, had a common shower together in our bathers and then got dressed in our separate change rooms. For me it was fun – we were all just the same, and there was never any flirting or interest between the girls and boys in our squad. We were just swimmers.

Any prior sexual experience was based around the disgust and dreadful shame from my relationship with my grandfather. What a surprise (not) that in my mid-teens I allowed myself to be compromised, abused and taken advantage of. I couldn't believe that someone might like me for me. I always felt I had to be a version of whatever a potential boyfriend wanted me to be. I didn't understand healthy boundaries and always acted from fear.

All these teen and young adult experiences continued to feed my shame and disgust. I knew I had to hide my true self even deeper if I was ever to be loved and accepted. I learned that unless I did what boys and men wanted me to do, I would never be considered girlfriend material.

Despite this, when I did get married, it was to a good man from a good family who seemed to love and accept each other. I knew he'd be a kind and good father. For the first time I felt safe, and if I could make him happy, perhaps I might find my happily ever after.

Oops – flawed thinking 101. Again, Dear Reader, fairy tales do not always come true.

My happy memories from our early years of marriage are also closely linked to feelings of sadness, hopelessness, emptiness, and of being completely alone. To the external world I was an accomplished leadership and empowerment consultant, I was totally involved in our children's lives, I had many friends and seemed to be happy and fully alive. Yet I felt constantly paralysed inside and beyond help. My continual thoughts of *I have to make them happy* drove every waking moment.

I felt as if I had a split personality. The person I knew myself to be had to be kept secret since I was so flawed and repellent. And if anyone were to discover my secret, I was sure they would feel deep disgust for me.

In my late thirties I knew with my whole heart that the lives of my husband and my two young children would be better off if I didn't exist. I couldn't sustain the happiness pretext any more.

Sure, they would grieve for a while, but I truly believed they would be happier and move on more easily if they weren't burdened with me in their lives. I had my exit all planned: my husband was taking the children to our beach house and I didn't intend to be alive when they arrived home. I'd even printed a note that read, *IF this door is closed when you come back from the beach, please do not open it until you have taken the kids to be safely somewhere else. Thank you.*

My plan started with me saying goodbye to the kids and my husband, and telling him I was going out for a walk at the park. I drove around the corner, parked the car in a side street, snuck back into our front garden and hid behind the hydrangeas, waiting for them to leave the house. While my husband was getting organised, for some reason both of our children spontaneously burst into joyous laughter. The deep belly laughs reached my soul and shocked me out of my pain. I realised that if I carried out my plan, I'd never hear that laughter again, and in that moment I took my life back.

I knocked and knocked on the outside wall of the house until my husband found me. This was the first time he really understood the severity of my depression and despair. And so began my decades-long journey along the path of training and taming the screaming inner demons that haunted me.

After the dramatic end of the last chapter, dare you read on? This is turning out to be like one of those *Choose Your Own Adventure* books I loved so much when I was young.

Oh, good. You are not skipping
this chapter. What a relief!

FFS, that wasn't on the birth plan

I'm getting ahead of myself – I did warn you that I might!

I'd always known I wanted to be a mother; I may even have been born with the words 'Mumma Bear – Beware' stamped on my head. I also knew I wanted to be nothing like my mum. That was my solid foundation. I was going to give my child all the love, the cuddles, the protection and attention I'd craved as a child, especially if I had a daughter. (Are you already thinking this isn't going to go so well? You'd be right – all is revealed in the *Gilmore Girls* chapter.)

My first pregnancy blessed me with a baby girl. When she was born she was pink and glowing and had the most magnificently shaped head because she came out backwards – yep, my girl was going to do the world her way.

I'd had quite a tough pregnancy with long months of anytime, anywhere, for-no-particular-reason vomiting, and I became very proficient at it. Someone must have pitied me at some stage and told me, 'The more the hormones, the stronger the baby.' I held onto that as my mantra. Of course

55

I'd suffer for this baby. My job was to bring this child safely into the world and there would always be magic, love and joy surrounding us. Even if it was at my personal expense.

I was due to give birth on 8 March. What an Aussie, I'd be in labour on Labour Day. My dad would've been so proud. (Spoiler alert – of course, it didn't happen that way.) Up until the last weeks of her incubation, my baby's movements had been relatively kind to me – no big, outrageous kicks or bits sticking into my various body parts; just some chilled and laid-back movement.

Two weeks before my due date things changed. I was sitting in the waiting room of my lovely obstetrician for a regular visit (he'll be known as My Obs Guy from now on) when my stomach started lurching as if a demon were trying to escape. Arms and legs poked out everywhere and there was smashing and bashing and tumble-turning in my stomach. It was sudden, only lasted a few seconds, and then it settled down again.

Oh, that was strange, I thought.

My Obs Guy finally welcomed me into his room. He introduced me to another doctor who was in training as part of his medical specialty. I consented for this doctor to have a feel (in a truly professional and honourable way) of my tummy. He palpated my belly then frowned. He felt again, and then in an uncertain tone suggested that the baby was presenting in a posterior breech position. He finished with a question mark.

I whipped my head around to My Obs Guy, who had told me the week before that the baby's head was well engaged. He gently shook his head in his wise manner, so of course I blurted out without thinking (as I am prone to do), 'Hahaha, you've failed.'

My Obs Guy stepped forward and gently palpated my tummy balloon and pulled out his fundus marker and tape measure. He asked if I had experienced any large movements lately, and I told him about my baby's recent tumble-turn antics in his waiting room.

To my horror (and embarrassment) he confirmed the posterior breech position and immediately ordered an ultrasound and x-ray to determine my internal hip measurements. My unborn child had decreed that a normal birth (what's with this 'normal' crap?) was not on the cards. Unless, of course, there was another tumble-turn with a half-twist sometime soon. As I left the room I mumbled an apology to the trainee doctor whom I had so soundly ridiculed thirty minutes earlier!

Since My Obs Guy was going away for a few days ('How rude!' we all scream in unison), I had to see the only other private obstetrics specialist in town, who we'll name Mr Alt Obs Guy. He would do the ultrasound and report back on the x-ray results.

Mr Alt Obs Guy was all sorts of 'Alt'. My Obs Guy wore a fancy suit and tie, gently palpated the 'tummy baby', and even put a dot with a pen on the top of my fundus to take accurate measurements of said 'tummy baby'. This was my impression of a professional.

Mr Alt Obs Guy was a round, jolly man with an unkempt frizzy mop of hair who rode around town on a bike with a basket on the front and flowers on the wheels. He wore overalls and a jaunty big bowtie. Yes, Dear Reader, alarm bells had started to ring. And not only did the two Obs Guys look dramatically different, but how they assessed the baby's position and the way they communicated were also dramatically different.

Alt Obs Guy had no marker pen in sight and there was no tape measure. In his jolly manner he wobbled my tummy around and said, 'There's about six pounds of body and half a pound of head in there.' I asked if the baby was still in a breech position. He said it was, but that was fine – the x-rays had shown that I had internal hips a truck could drive through (his exact words) and I would have no trouble delivering a baby this size as long as I didn't go over my due date. No stress at all here, Pam. But how was I to convince the baby to arrive on time when it had a mind of its own?

A few days later, when My Obs Guy was conveniently back in town, I went into early labour. Excellent! The baby was arriving a week early and would still fit through my truck-sized hips.

I was totally prepared. I had my birth plan, My Obs Guy, and a midwife friend who was going to be our birth assistant (to look after both my husband and me during the labour – oh, how progressive for the mid-80s!), I also had a wonderful attitude and knew that every pain was a step closer to unwrapping the greatest present ever. In comparison to the horror stories I'd heard, I truly believed my labour was going to be straightforward, even if quite painful at times, and I was ready for the journey towards the climaxing event – the delivery. Thankfully, there was no Dr Google back then to advise me on the seriousness and complexity of a breech birth.

After a few hours of an intense progression towards birth, I declared in a panic to my midwife and husband that I wanted to do a poo! My midwife took a look and said, 'That's no poo – that's the baby coming.'

Since I wasn't in a delivery room at this time, my team embarked on frantic activity. They transferred me to a wheelchair and my husband started pushing me down an embarrassingly long hall. Not wanting to sit on my baby's bottom, I teetered on the very edge of the chair while our support person held my legs way up in the air. (Sorry about the visual, Dear Reader!)

In the delivery room there was no time left for pain meds because the birth was imminent. I was positioned with my legs up in stirrups and my nethers exposed. By now the birthing plan had well and truly gone out the window. Trying to be useful, my husband started coaching me to breathe deeply. He took the breathing exercises a little too literally, however, and nearly passed out from hyperventilation, which I found quite amusing.

Just as My Obs Guy was about to deliver the baby, bottom first, the delivery room magically filled with people in medical uniforms. I later found out that vaginal breech births were uncommon and could be complex and dangerous, and that's why everyone available crowded in for the show. For many, it was their first experience of a vaginal breech birth. At this stage, with my legs akimbo, my care factor was seriously below zero.

Apparently My Obs Guy had done a lot of training in the UK and had extensive experience in this type of birth. Perhaps I should have asked him exactly how much experience and how successful the births were, but I had complete faith in him.

I was told to push, and push I did. Because I had a New Age birthing-plan I asked my friend to hold up a mirror so I could watch. I gave a good push then grunted, 'That's so ugly!'

My Obs Guy said, 'It's only the baby's bottom, Pam.'

To which I exclaimed, 'No, not that – my face!'

My Obs Guy (not known for his humour) said, 'No one is looking at your face, Pam!' This was received with chuckles and suppressed laughter from the stands.

Soon after that my baby was born and someone said, 'Congratulations, you have a son!'

Taking him in my arms, my instant thought was, *He has no penis, but I will love him anyway!*

But the statement was quickly reversed – 'No! It's a girl, it's a girl!'

Because my baby presented with her little bottom down, finding her own escape route, her 'girly bits' had become swollen and were temporarily mistaken for 'boy bits'. (Translation: her labial lips were swollen and temporarily mistaken for testicles. You get to choose which version you like better.)

No matter what her girly bits looked like, not having her head engaged in my pelvis meant Rosie (Rosemary) Joy was born with a delicate, perfectly shaped head that was admired by many, especially by the family of the lady I was sharing a room with. She had delivered a son two weeks past her due date, had a very long labour and gave birth to an enormous baby boy with a particularly moulded head. Her son, who was in a humidicrib because of the traumatic birth, was nearly twice the size and weight of my little Rosie. I felt a bit sad for her but that was greatly diminished by my total delight at all the coo-ing and compliments I received for my little rosy-cheeked girl. (She was not named Rosemary because she had rosy cheeks, although that would have been the perfect ending to my story.)

Those days were the start of the 'Breast is Best' philosophy and feeding on demand. The baby's needs had to come first, and I was fortunate to be a milk-making machine. I seemed to have a permanent appendage in Rosie, and I was love-struck. This was my purpose – to be this child's everything: her protector, her provider, her source of comfort, and of course she would have an innate sense of my self-sacrificing love. I quickly became overprotective and didn't trust anyone else with her, including my husband.

I was in a wonderful playgroup of lovely women who all had children slightly older than my baby girl. My greatest wish for Rosie was that she would grow up to be a strong, independent woman no one would ever be able to take advantage of, and that she would have a voice and be heard – so what better people to learn from than mothers who were a couple of steps ahead of me? I was an eager sponge, soaking up their experiences, advice and guidance because I HAD to be the best. And what this looked like, Dear Reader, was a mother and daughter who were best friends, closer than humanly possible, sharing every moment with delight and joy. Do I detect a few dry retches? Some knowing nods? Or some 'FFS, Pammy – what are you setting yourself up for?'

Many years of therapy have been required to untangle the web of pain I experienced because I was so determined for my children to know they were loved. It was my duty, and my duty alone, to protect them from all sorts of harm – just like a superhero. I could do it; I knew I could. Until I couldn't. And then I got lost somewhere, somehow back into the only reality I was certain of – making it my responsibility to make people happy.

FFS, I have ocular toxoplasmosis!

When my beautiful baby girl was about four months old, I noticed something strange happening to my right eye. It felt as if there was a big blob of gloop in it and I couldn't see very well. I tried to blink it away. That didn't work, yet every time I looked in the mirror there was nothing there. I winked my way through the week, hoping it would get better but, of course, as they say, 'Hope is not a method'!

I was living in Wangaratta, Country Victoria, at this stage. My doctor, Kate, was very good, popular and in high demand, so my appointment was not for a few days. By the time I went my eye still looked perfectly fine but inside it felt as though it was going to pop right out of its socket.

After lots of pleasantries, my appointment went something like this:

'Um, Kate, I think there is something wrong with my right eye.'

She asked a few questions, got out her eye-thingy (which is the correct medical terminology, of course), peered into my right eye, then said, 'Come with me.'

I thought this was a bit strange, but it became even stranger when she opened the broom closet and beckoned me inside with her. She got out her eye-thingy again and kept examining both my eyes.

'Hmm,' she said, 'I think you're right.'

We went back to her office where she made a phone call, and within an hour I was sitting in the waiting room of the town's ophthalmologist. The words *eye pressure, retina, serious, you're right* and *urgent* were vying for space in my head.

The eventual diagnosis was ocular toxoplasmosis. (Ohh – sounds toxic, doesn't it?) There were three active sites of toxoplasmosis – parasitic cysts – embedded in my retina. They had apparently been there for a long time and the hypothesis was that the hormone imbalance from my pregnancy had triggered this activation. I was also told that cysts could form in my brain, ears, lungs and muscles, and this information was accompanied with the perfunctory words, 'But let's not worry about that until we have to.' Words that only served to make me more worried than I already was. I'm sure you know the feeling, Dear Reader.

At this stage my cheeky little cysts were situated close to my optic nerve, causing a massive build-up of pressure. If left untreated, I could permanently lose the sight in my right eye.

The immediate treatment involved a cortisone injection

into my eyeball. My first thought was whether I'd be able to continue to breastfeed Rosie or not. I was told there was little likelihood the cortisone would pass through the breast milk and that this was just the first step until they could decide which antiparasitic treatment I should take.

They said the injection wouldn't be painful and they were correct. Even though there are few (if any) pain receptors on the surface of the eyeball, they put in numbing drops first. The worst bit was having to have my eye open. They instructed me to look away, but the needle still registered as an incoming weapon in my peripheral vision.

I wasn't supposed to drive home but I had Rosie and she was cranky, and 'It's a country township for heaven's sake.' Besides, it never occurred to me to actually ask someone for help – a recurring theme in my life. So I drove home with my right eye closed (thankfully we didn't live far from the hospital). I had to wear sunglasses for the rest of the day, but apart from that my face looked no different from usual.

I remember asking the ophthalmologist if I could wear an eye patch like a pirate, but he said there was really no need. I desperately wanted a patch. I wanted someone to ask if I was okay. Or if I needed anything. I wanted people to know something was wrong because I was really, really scared.

And thus began my lonely journey of knowing something was wrong with me even though I didn't look any different.

I can easily recall my thoughts from this time because they still recur today. Thoughts such as: *Nothing good comes from asking; They'll think you can't cope; You're weak; You should be able to do this yourself*; and worst of all: *They'll think you're needy.*

After about four months of treatment with an antiparasitic drug my eye returned to normal, leaving only a small amount of scarring around the cyst.

A few months later I found out that I didn't have some sort of stomach flu but was about ten weeks pregnant. When I hit twelve weeks my eye symptoms returned. I went straight back to the ophthalmologist and yep, there was a parasite party happening in my eye all over again. The ophthalmologist was quite sure the baby would have toxo antibodies so there was no danger from that angle, but the drugs I'd need were another story and the pregnancy would have to be terminated. On the flip side, as before, if left untreated I could potentially lose the sight in my right eye, and there was the ever-present possibility that outbreaks could occur elsewhere in my body.

For me, the decision was easy. If I lost my sight, I had another eye. My mum was born with a blood clot in her eye and she did very well with just one eye. I could too.

For my husband, that sort of thinking didn't compute. His logic was that the danger to me was too great and we could always have another baby. But the thought of aborting my baby was horrendous to me, especially with pregnancy hormones racing through my body. We were at a crossroads. I was not going to budge. And he was not prepared to adjust his logic. It was a very difficult time.

Luckily – and I use that word very loosely – I miscarried my baby a few days before we had to make the final decision to either abort and save my vision or not abort and potentially lose sight in one eye. My husband was relieved that God had solved our problem. For him, it was sad but was meant to be.

I can't describe the incredible loneliness I felt after the death of my baby. The feeling wasn't only physical, it was spiritual. People tried to console me. They said how sad it was that I'd lost a baby. I didn't lose my baby. He was never going to turn up in Lost and Found somewhere. My baby died. No one seemed to acknowledge this. My baby died. And I have never forgotten him.

My miscarriage occurred the day before a friend from Sydney turned up on our doorstep in despair and needing help. So I just got on with the job of supporting her and trying to make her feel better. Soon after she left I was sitting outside with my back against the clothesline, howling, rocking back and forth, feeling shattered and totally alone. My logical husband popped his head out to check if I was okay and to see if I wanted the outside light left on or not. He was and is a kind man, but he was totally clueless about empathy. It didn't make sense to him that a potentially unhealthy baby could cause this level of emotion a week or so after the miscarriage.

Under the bright stars of Country Victoria, sitting outside all alone, I decided my baby was a boy and that night I named him Ollie. Not Oliver, but Ollie, my special name for my special baby. I told him he would always have a part of my heart. And thirty-five years on, he still does.

After my miscarriage I was back on antiparasitic drugs. Thankfully these drugs were sponsored by the hospital because they were really expensive. Since I was no longer pregnant, the doctors thought that, as a bonus, I could now take a large dose of cortisone orally, which would not only be much better than a cortisone poke in the eye with a big needle, it would also bring the swelling down more quickly.

I wasn't told that cortisone could create mood swings, raise anxiety and impact mental health, so I thought my mood swings were because I wasn't coping with the death of Ollie. Of course I couldn't reveal how I was feeling since everyone else was over it. Remember my motto: never, ever ask for help.

Dear Reader, if someone you know has
been impacted by a miscarriage,
please remember this chapter and
be gentle with them.

FFS, I'm scared

I became pregnant again when my gorgeous baby girl was thirteen months old. It was unexpected and unplanned. And I was scared. Would the toxo come back? Would I have to go through the whole Ollie experience again? Did I have the strength to go through another miscarriage? We waited fourteen weeks before telling anyone and they were so happy with the news. I pulled up my happy pants and got on with the job of growing my baby, even through the fear that something could still go wrong.

Thankfully, my third pregnancy was toxo-free, although I did, once again, spend the first four months vomiting. I was relieved to be so sick because 'The more I vomit, the stronger the hormones, the healthier the baby.' This old wives' tale gave me great comfort in those early months, just as it had when I was pregnant with Rosie.

The baby was due on 26 January – Australia Day. My husband was excited to have a little Aussie baby and My Obs Guy was taking a week's leave on the 27th, so I felt under some pressure to perform. We didn't know the sex of the baby since gender reveals were not a thing in those days, but whether it was Ollie or this new baby, I was scared to have a baby boy. I only knew about baby girls and was clueless about how to manage a little penis. Besides, I'd already chosen the name for my girl child – Philippa Jean. I was going to have two girls, called Rosie and Pip.

I started having contractions as planned like a Good Aussie Day Mumma. I was eager to hurry them along and thought if I went for a brisk walk, that might help. Much to my husband's dismay, I even tried running down a few small hills and finished with a round of squat jumps, trying to jolt my baby out. I'm not sure this is a recommended 'bring on more contractions' methodology but something worked. Contractions started coming every four to five minutes and off we went in the car to the hospital 1.5 kilometres away.

The contractions stopped the minute I got there! When My Obs Guy examined me, he asked if I wanted to have the baby today. (Meaning he was going away the next day, I suppose.) 'Of course,' was my response. He suggested he induce the labour by having a drip inserted. I didn't really want to go down this intervention route, but I agreed. First, because I wanted my baby to come out while My Obs Guy was around, and second, this baby was nicely cooked already. Just as they were setting up the drippy thing, I had a massive contraction.

My Obs Guy thought I was faking it (he knew me a bit by now) but I promised I wasn't. So he gave me five minutes to have another one – he was timing – and just like that, the fear of having a drippy thing attached to me kicked me into regular labour pains. The birthing game was ON.

I have a strange response to pain – I tend to laugh a lot and verbally describe how big the pain is. As the labour pains grew more intense I started laughing and saying things like, 'Ohhhh – hahahaha this is big, hahahaha – this is REALLY big.' I didn't mean to entertain others, but I'm pretty sure I did.

As a new-age mother, I was going to have a birth that was as natural as possible – no stirrups this time!

Someone had told me that relaxed fingers equals a relaxed vag. This sounded like a good idea, so in the final stages of labour, when I was no longer laughing, my focus was on wiggling my fingers in all sorts of ways. There I was, leaning over a bean bag, arms against the wall and wiggling my fingers like a crazed woman as I attempted to birth this baby in a relaxed way.

It was around 11.45pm and I'd been in uncomfortable labour for about thirty minutes. My well-intentioned and loving husband asked if I could push a little harder so we could have an Australia Day baby. As you know, back then I was not a swearing person, but his comment was enough for the word fuck to just pop out of my mouth, along with a few other colourful words.

But my body had already decided to take over and I had no control anymore. At one point the pain was so severe I tried to suck the baby's head back in, but my body would have nothing to do with that nonsense. A few minutes later, our baby arrived and I held my little Aussie Day boy.

When I held him for the first time my only thoughts were, *A boy! A boy! I have always wanted a boy!* All my fears had been replaced by overwhelming love for this little baby with a penis. I knew I would work it all out and my heart seemed to triple its capacity to love.

Since he was born on Australia Day, for most of his childhood Larry received a special birthday card each year along with a badge from the head of the Australia Day Committee, plus invitations to march in the Australia Day Parade as part of the 26ers and to attend an afternoon tea with cake at Government House. We attended the parade as observers twice, I think. We never went to eat the cake.

The highlight for Larry came before the parade on one of the days we went. A friend of my husband's was in the Harley Davidson Returned Vietnam Vets, who would lead the main parade, and he invited our seven-year-old boy onto his huge Harley. Larry straddled the bike wearing his gift – an original HD bandanna purchased in the USA. I still remember his cheeky smile. This could never be outdone, and we didn't attend again.

Who would have thought that, years later, Larry's birthday would become a complex social, emotional and political issue? In so many ways I am thrilled to live in Australia, but I also know the continued pain this day signifies for our First Peoples. How could they even consider celebrating a day when their traditional lands were stolen and their ancestors categorised as part of the Flora and Fauna Act until 1967?

For now, I resolve my internal conflict about the birthdate of my son by knowing that 26 January signifies The International Day of the Birth of the Baby Boy called Larry (Laurence) Charles. And in my opinion, that event deserves an Australian public holiday.

I am an advocate for equity, inclusion and diversity for others. Yet I have no idea about what I want for myself and have no real plans for my future. However, I also know that I am on a lifelong journey. And it is totally okay for me to not have all the answers right now. And to accept that I may never have all of the answers!

Ohhhhh, I am uncomfortable right now with the fact that despite all this lifelong learning, I might die and still not really understand the mysteries between life experiences, life lessons and spiritual evolution. Am I just an advanced chimp with an overwhelming need to go on a search, like Bilbo Baggins in *The Hobbit?*

FFS, I'm back on the toxo wagon

I was toxo-free until Larry abruptly stopped breastfeeding at ten months old. What was it with both babies rejecting me at this age? Despite all my coaxing he was, like, 'speak to the hand', which was firmly clamped in his mouth when I offered my milk. Whether my breast milk knew I had toxo or was about to get it, who knows.

This time it was much more acute. Those little toxo-critters were at a full-on rage party! It was time to call in the big guns again. As I was no longer breastfeeding (unlike with Rosie), the ophthalmologist chose an intense, short-term chemo drug and big bazooka levels of cortisone. My eyesight got better, but my emotions, anxiety, anger, sleep deprivation and manic busyness increased tenfold. It was scary.

This time I made an appointment to see another doctor, who was also in our friendship circle. I remember I walked into his office, gave him a smile and then thumped my hand on his desk and yelled, 'What the fuck is happening to me? I am such a happy person. Am I going mad?'

He looked up the drug combination I was taking and told me that a common side effect of this particular combination was that old lemon – clinical depression. I left the doctor's office bewildered and with the first of many prescriptions for antidepressants.

And so arrived the last nail in my socially acceptable life: 'My brain is damaged, I have the Big D-word, and even worse, I need to take – drumroll please – antidepressants.' Yippee!

(Later in this roller-coaster ride of a story you'll find out how I was on the wrong medication for over ten years, and the answer the GPs had when I was still not feeling better was to increase the dosage of a drug that was not working – ahhhh, the irony.)

Back in the late eighties there was a perception that anyone with depression must have some sort of weakness or personality flaw. Besides, what in the world did I have to be depressed about? I had two gorgeous children, was married to a very nice and kind man and, on the surface, had a great life. When I tried to reach out to friends they said, 'Are you sure? That doesn't sound right,' or 'Don't worry, we all get a bit down,' or 'Try not to think about it – it will only make it worse,' and my all-time favourite: 'Just think happy thoughts – you'll be fine.'

I felt incredibly alone, misunderstood and broken, with the added shame of having something that no one wanted to know about. This was the start of my journey of learning to live a lie. When asked how I was, I learnt very quickly to say, 'I'm fine, thanks,' and I became the master of great conversations because I was always sooooo interested in other people's days, lives, children and even their despair, all to avoid having to risk either exposing myself or having to lie outright yet again: 'No, really – I'm fine.'

At this stage I was also unaware that the potential side effects of taking antidepressants included a complete loss of any sexual drive or desire, massive weight gain and disturbing dreams. I had all of these – a Super-Sized Big Mac of side effects – and they lasted for decades. The massive weight gain in particular added to my complete lack of self-esteem and self-worth.

This year's therapy is really focusing
on the PTSD aspect of my mental health
Big Mac. As my psychiatrist said, 'You
certainly must have asked for a spiritual
journey of "one with the lot".' Seems that
I've had quite a few soul lessons to learn
this time and I must have said,
'Bring them on!'

FFS, Pam, don't call it the fat chapter

Today I'm trying my hardest to reframe the shit out of my constant companion, the one that whispers, yells or screams hysterically in my brain, 'You are not only fat, you are disgusting.'

When I told my gorgeous book coach Kathy, during a weekly Zoom call, that I was going to be working on The Fat Chapter, she gave me one of those strange looks. She paused as if she wanted to contribute something but also wanted it to be my idea. With her head tilted slightly and her eyes focused on me, she took a breath and said, 'Maybe …?'

Bum. That look and that tone usually mean she thinks I need to reconsider what I'm writing about, or at least how I'm approaching it. Her suggestion of reframing the title to something less self-deprecating will hopefully allow me to gain some valuable insights.

She's right; I will always go down the most self-deprecating route. Vomiting up my truths but not adding a tincture of wisdom of what I've learned. So this is my attempt to address a painful topic in a more enlightened way.

I wondered whether I might have Body Dysmorphic Disorder (BDD to its friends). I took a little side trip and asked the omnipotent Dr Google what 'morphic' (*a specific shape or form*) and 'dys' (*something bad, ill, abnormal, impaired*) meant. I thought that since I have a fat, abnormal, impaired, damaged body I must have BDD. I then found an online BDD quiz and scored 52 out of 72 with a 'highly likely' BDD diagnosis.

Seriously??? Does that mean I now have another few letters to add to my already impressive, acronym-heavy mental health diagnosis?

When I saw my psychiatrist after starting this chapter, we discussed my latest Dr Google-informed self-prognosis. He made it very clear that I do NOT have Body Dysmorphic Disorder. BDD is an extreme distortion of body image (looking into a mirror and seeing your face twisted, or an anorexic who is about to die of starvation still thinking they are fat). Nope – I don't have that and I don't want that!

We both agreed that I have a powerful negative body image. Well, that's a no-brainer – 'I hate my body' equals negative body image.

(For those of you desperate to offer solutions for how I could solve this problem – thank you for your kind thoughts. However, please indulge me a while longer so I can shine some light on my brand of body shame.)

My psychiatrist and I both know there are many things

in my life that contribute to the intensity of my negative body image. In this session we started to explore the times I've believed I'm a lesser person because of my size. Of course, we'd addressed this in past sessions and I'd probably nodded as if I was taking it in, while inside all I heard was 'blah blah blah' because I KNEW I was disgusting. This time I was ready to listen and really start challenging my fundamental beliefs about my body.

As an aside, this ended up being an eight-tissue visit. The number of tissues used indicates the intensity of the tears shed per session. My Unbroken Tissue Record currently stands at ten very soggy tissues, a record that was established years ago. So much progress, Pammy! So much!

My story of knowing something was wrong with my body started with a nickname I was given by my uncle. He adored my older sister, Elizabeth. She was undoubtedly the family favourite as a child – the first-born granddaughter for both sets of grandparents, very cute and by all reports an excellent baby and a crowd pleaser. My uncle had blessed her with a cute moniker based on her early attempts at saying her name, Biff.

When she was nearly three years old, I came along. I don't know much about my baby days but I was told that when I was about ten months old and taking my first steps, I plopped down on my bum and sat awkwardly on my ankle, breaking that sucker! I was also well-fed and chubby, if the few photos of me are anything to go by. Not being able to crawl or move much at all for a few extra months may have contributed to my cute, chubby thighs and my uncle proclaiming that I be forever crowned Pudden Jo, just like a fat little pudding.

Not only was my sister the adored one, she also had the well-behaved, good-girl role totally nailed. So from as young as I can remember, I engaged in a number of ways to become the centre of attention instead of her. My dad made people laugh and that seemed like a good thing to do. But when I tried to make people laugh I was told not to be a show-off. Then I tried to do the same things my sister did, like skipping, only to be told how clumsy I was.

Then I tried to impress Dad's parents by reciting the first fourteen books of the Old Testament off by heart. The rhythm still haunts me: Genesis, Exodus, Leviticus, Numbers, Deuteronomy ... all the way to Ruth. I'd stop there because that was my mother's name, then I'd take a deep breath and continue until I got to First and Second Chronicles. I thought I had nailed it; not even my sister could go that far! My grandmother would test me each time she visited. I'd confidently get to First and Second Chronicles then forget the rest and have to start again. Imagine my deflation at being told there were twenty-seven books in the Old Testament but I could try again another time. I gave up – attention was much easier to gain by getting into trouble, receiving a quick smack and being told to leave the room.

I don't think my grandparents even went to church and I can't remember why I thought it was a good idea, or even where I learned the sequence. The only religious thing my family ever did –apart from the Mum drop-and-run Sunday School punishments – was to eat smoked cod on Good Friday. I still gag at the memory – they were never good Fridays for me.

Back to the Pudden Jo story. (Yes, I digressed, but I'm back now.)

Even though I was a fantastic swimmer and state champion in a couple of events and, as a result, fit, healthy, strong and muscular, Pudden Jo haunted me into my pre-teens. I thought I'd made my discomfort clear to my uncle but this seemed to make it even more fun for him and he used it every time he saw me. In the end it was easier to be naughty and sent from the room than to be in his presence.

I didn't see him much as a teenager and the name dropped away. I don't recall having many body issues during high school because of my high level of training and commitment to swimming. Even so, I was bullied mercilessly – but that's a completely different kettle of fish and will require another whole book. Suffice to say it significantly contributed to my shattered self-esteem and feelings of safety.

When I was fifteen my parents thought it'd be a good idea

(WTF!) for me to apply for a one-year Rotary exchange to the Philippines. This was when the entire country was under the Marcos government with martial law. My application was successful and my parents sent me off with no idea who I'd be staying with or what the arrangements were for my year abroad.

I got off the plane, a tall, athletic teenager wearing the look of the Australian 70s – hot pants (short shorts) and clogs – that made my legs look even longer. Dear Reader, as you gasp and question *WTF were you thinking* – the answer is I was not. We had no cultural briefings from Rotary before we left – that was not a thing way back then – so I wasn't aware of how inappropriate my clothing was. I also didn't know that Filipino women wore shorts or long skirts with a tee-shirt to swim at public beaches, so when I went for my first swim in my skin-tight Speedos I must have looked nearly nude to them.

My clothing made me a beacon for male attention – from experienced boys older than me and even some of the Rotarians. I was sexually repressed and hated the attention my body seemed to attract and what it made men want to do to me.

After some very uncomfortable discussions and unwanted advances (and at the insistence of the mother of my host family), my contemporary clothing was replaced with loose coverings and long pants. A tee-shirt and shorts weren't pleasant to swim in, so I avoided swimming as best I could.

After never having eaten rice before in my life, I was now eating it three times a day and drinking soft-drinks with every meal because the water quality was so poor even when boiled – I can't remember ever drinking water over there. But what a bonus for 15-year-old Pam – at home we only had soft-drinks on birthdays or special occasions. I'd also gone cold turkey on my intensive swimming regime and so I gained weight. Lots of weight. And quickly.

I became the butt of jokes. The word for fat in Tagalog is *tambok*. How very funny then to call me *Pambok*. And that is how I was referred to for the last six months of my year away. Another joke was, 'When you arrived, they all said – "Ooooooh, legs". Now they all say – "Arrrrrgh, logs"'.

The final insult in this Philippine tale of woe was unexpected. I hadn't contemplated how my transformed body would be received when I arrived back in Australia.

For example, the look on the face of a boy called Chook who I'd been writing to when I was away. Bless his cotton socks, he was excited to see me arrive home and his dad brought him to the airport to meet me off the plane. I'll never forget his look of disgust when he finally recognised me beneath a mass of extra kilos. It was so awkward and embarrassing. He and his dad left very quickly and I avoided him whenever I could at school, never really speaking to him again.

Most people thought I'd be the same person, or an even better version of myself. My life was expected to be business as usual, and of course that meant a return to swimming. Before I left Australia I was in the fast lanes – the lanes where all the successful swimmers trained: the Champion Lanes. Then there were the Baby Lanes, for aspiring juniors who might one day move up to Champion Lanes, or champions recovering from injury. And finally there were the Try Hard Lanes that everyone else fell into. I used to snigger at the swimmers in those lanes because I knew they'd never reach success. I wasn't an injured champion – I was just fat and unfit and in bathers three sizes bigger than those I'd had before I left, so the Try Hard Lanes were where I belonged.

Even though I lost most of the weight relatively quickly (only eating lettuce leaves, apples and celery for days at a time), it didn't take me long to understand that I was never going to be as good at swimming as I used to be. There was no encouragement and no opportunity for counselling, so after a year I just gave up and pretended not to care. But of course I did care – I felt such a disappointment and felt I had no worth.

Fast forward about ten years (yes, speeding along, Dear Reader). I had wanted to be a doctor. However, my dad told me that being a teacher was a good profession for a woman, so I graduated with a degree in applied science (human movement) and a diploma in education (physical education).

The irony of my early career choice and lifestyle doesn't escape me, and I wonder if I was subconsciously trying to prove to everyone that I could be fit again, that I could succeed.

My first year of teaching is a bit of a long story (but when are any of my stories not long, you may be thinking) and, yes, there was drama involved. One of the schools in the state of Victoria that I asked NOT to be posted to was Preston Technical School. By a twist of fate, that's exactly where I ended up. And FFS it was an initiation by fire! I had no idea what I was doing and the students were a tough crowd.

I taught PE there for two uncomfortable years since I had no other options and was desperate to have my own money so I could escape my parents' home ... and also being able to eat was nice. A couple of friends and I mastered the skill of power drinking after work most days while playing Space Invaders at the local pub. (I am delighted to tell you that I maintain a lovely friendship with one of my Space Invader gangsters and we are both somewhat respectable people!)

I – and my liver – were joyful to leave Preston Tech at the end of 1981 to take up an amazing opportunity to work at an outdoor education camp near the snowfields of Falls Creek. During summer I taught fifteen- to sixteen-year-old kids rock climbing, abseiling, bush walking, bushcraft, rope courses and, in winter, cross-country and downhill skiing. I started running up and down the steep local roads. I was fit, healthy and competent and I loved my life. I even fell in love with a young man who worked at a school at the base of the mountain and who I met at the local ski club.

My future husband was gentle, a family man and he LOVED me. I was his ideal woman: outdoorsy, active, interesting and fun. We went ski-touring and bush walking, and organised group bike rides that could last for days. We skied in Canada and the USA.

I moved off the mountain to Wangaratta so we could spend more time together. I taught PE at the local high school and he taught PE at the local technical school. We got engaged, then married. We bought a house – an extreme do-er upper. We were young and enthusiastic, life was good and I even felt good within myself.

After the birth of my children I became conscious of the fact that, unlike all the other recent mothers, I seemed to be the only one who didn't have their weight just fall off while breastfeeding. I hardly had time to eat properly and it seemed like every cell of my body was being sucked out of my nipples, but the weight and my saggy belly didn't instantly disappear as it had for everyone else.

And remember my toxo eye? Weight gain was one of the side effects of the oral cortisone I was taking, so not only did I not lose weight while breastfeeding, once I stopped it piled on even more as a result of my medication. AND the small print noted a 'do you want fries with that' side effect – clinical depression. So, I upsized my order and took anti-depressants. Guess what goes with those little suckers? Weight gain!

The doubts crept in and I started body-shaming the woman I saw in the mirror. And then the game of pretence began. I pretended I was okay. I pretended I didn't hate myself. I pretended I was in control. I didn't tell anyone. I refused to see a psychiatrist because that would prove my greatest fear – that I really was a nut job.

That thwarted suicide plan when my children were in their early school years brought the realisation of how totally lost I was. Finally, I had to contemplate admitting that I needed help. And so began my decades-long journey to acceptance of who I am – weight and all. It's still a work in progress.

It seems bizarre that almost everyone I know hopes and prays for my recovery so the veil can be lifted to reveal the real me. I've heard all their solutions – think happy thoughts, commit to a routine, exercise more, lose some weight, change medication, change psychiatrists, see more psychiatrists, stop seeing psychiatrists, give your problems up to God, think logically, join a club, distract yourself, don't worry so much, sew something, reflect on all the positives, blah, blah, fucking blah.

But what if this *is* the real me? Many people don't understand that recovery will mean leaving behind life as I know it; that a venture into the world of wellness is uncertain and unfamiliar. It's scary. When I start heading that way I become anxious and irritable and want to retreat back to my old depressed self. I have no idea what to expect, especially since I have trouble remembering what I was like before the depression began. As the symptoms of depression improve or go away, will they leave a hole in the way I think and act and view the world?

FFS, I'm FITH

After being found virtually paralysed and hiding in our front garden on that fateful day, I still believed I was the problem – I was a bad wife, a bad mother, a fraud at work. As it happened, my husband and I both agreed I needed help to be 'fixed'. Visiting a psychiatrist was out of the question because that would be even more evidence that my brain was totally fucked, so I had a few sessions with various psychologists instead. This got me nowhere because I truly believed the dark thoughts running through my brain could never be revealed to anyone, especially a psychologist. My medications were increased. I started to think I had a split personality, and that if only I could hide it better then I'd be fine.

Finally I found a psychologist who seemed lovely. I started to share a little bit – not the real me but the dark side of me, because if I did she'd know I was damaged and I'd be institutionalised. We were just starting to break through my impenetrable defensive wall when she got pregnant. She told me she had found me a psychiatrist who would treat me as a person and not a diagnosis. She was concerned about the anti-depressants I was taking and he would be able to monitor them. He was also one of the few who did not subscribe to fucking psychobabble but engaged in psychotherapy (talk therapy).

Luckily, yet tragically, when I finally got to see him after three months on the waiting list I found out I'd been on the wrong medication for over eight years and was currently taking a near toxic level. Each time I'd changed doctors no one had ever questioned that maybe I was on the incorrect medication. From the psychiatrist I learned that the antidepressant I'd been taking in ever-increasing doses was linked to suicide in women and was generally more effective with men! Ha – who would've thunk that!

The other horrible news for me was that there was no easy fix. Even the best psychiatrists in the world can't predict the chemical imbalance in your brain. They have only their best educated guess. I fantasise that one day there'll be a blood test of the brain that accurately predicts which chemicals are lacking and therefore which drug combo will balance the brain chemicals effectively so they can function in the best possible way. Until then, it is all experimentation and a juggling act.

I'd been blaming my depression purely on a chemical imbalance triggered by the medication taken when I had toxo eye. I hadn't even considered the psychological factors that might be contributing to my mental health issues – all the suppressed incidents from my past, for example – thinking that they had no impact on my mental health and the best thing to do was just move on.

In the early years of my treatment my psychiatrist tried a number of different prescriptions and combinations to try to minimise the debilitating impact this disease (dis-ease) had on my life. Which brings me to the other thing that no one tells you: when you start taking any sort of depression medication, it will be four to six weeks before you feel a difference – if any. And then you have to give the medication an opportunity to work its magic, which is usually six months.

Oh, the irony. Taking new medications when you know you may not feel any better for four to six weeks, and then, even if you don't feel any better, knowing you still have to stay on them for six months – unless they're having massive side effects beyond the stock-standard ones of weight gain, a loss of libido (which is a bit of an oxymoronic side effect as in my case I had no interest in my libido anyway) and insomnia (yay – let's add a sleeping tablet with that).

Finally, when the psychiatrist realises that this drug is not syncing with your brain and the dark thoughts are not getting better, you have to wean off it for two weeks – yes, two weeks – before you can start a new medication, in the hope this one will hit the jackpot.

With each medication following the same failed pattern, I was left feeling as though I'd never be fixed.

But because my psychiatrist did good old talk therapy, and because I wasn't 'fixed' yet, I was stuck with seeing him regularly and we started to unpack my life. This was a very dark period as I tried to grapple with who I was, or who I thought I should be (I now have a pet aversion to this self-flagellating, toxic word 'should'), and it made me feel even emptier because I had no idea who I would be if I couldn't make others happy.

We spoke about my marriage, about parenting and about my great fears that my children might end up like me – FITH (another acronym I have gifted myself: Fucked In The Head). We talked about my fears of being uncovered as a fraud in my professional life, my fixation on having to get everything right, my shame about being defective, and my confession that every day I felt as if I was living a lie, wading through quicksand just to get things done. I was petrified that the true me had no real redeeming qualities.

My feelings were so intense that I couldn't explain them to my husband, who obviously cared and supported me – at least at the start. Of course, way back then neither of us had any knowledge of how I could best be supported anyway.

Slowly, I began to reconnect with my dysfunctional

childhood. I started to give voice to the pain I thought I'd buried so far into the Earth that it was likely to pop up on the other side of the world somewhere in China. As my story unfolded and the darkness surfaced, my depression grew more intense.

The other thing they don't tell you, when you open up to your therapist, is that you feel very vulnerable. After each session I felt raw, exposed and broken, but I had to go home, back to my family life where I retreated into a world of pretence, the world of the Smiling Depressive.

During the few times I did share parts of my shameful history and my deep despair, my husband didn't know what to do. He totally loved the cheery, athletic, dynamic woman he'd married fifteen years earlier and he wanted her back. Or at the very least he wanted to keep the woman I'd been struggling for years to pretend to be. For the first few years he gave me space and time. What I really needed was compassion, hugs and reassurance.

When I didn't seem to be getting better, he thought perhaps my psychiatrist wasn't doing a good enough job and suggested I seek a second opinion, an option he shared frequently not only with me but also with my nearest and dearest. Perhaps they could convince me to see someone else. But I didn't want this, and I think it may have been one of the very first times in our relationship that I didn't comply with his wishes. I am sure his suggestion came from a place of love, but all it did was drive me more deeply away from him.

Trying my hardest to appear normal was exhausting and is one of the reasons I started to drink in secret. This was NOT a recommendation from my psychiatrist. But when I drank, for a time my brain was numb and that was a relief, so I persisted with this method of coping. My self-harming also started around this time.

My psychiatrist mentioned that exercise could reduce levels of anxiety and raise the serotonin levels – the happy hormone. My husband thought so too. He was a fit, healthy man who loved exercise and he seemed to commit to his routine with even more enthusiasm when I began withdrawing from life. Dear Reader, we know the woman he married had been fit and healthy, so he reminded me of all the potential benefits – how I could feel better, look better and get better.

How could I tell this man that my mind was so distorted with self-loathing and disgust that I thought people would want to vomit when they saw my body with all its extra fat flapping up and down as I walked?

I genuinely wanted to stop feeling like a total disappointment to him, so I came up with an elaborate scheme to get him off my back and prove I was trying to help myself. My Exercise Survival Scheme (ESS) went something like this:

* Get dressed into exercise pants, tee-shirt and runners.

* Say I was going to drive to one of my favourite parks and walk around it.

* Tell him I should be back in an hour.

* Then drive to a street a suburb away that I knew he would never come down, and either have a sleep, read a book I kept hidden in my car, or just sit on the grass under some random tree.

* Before driving back, exercise in a ridiculous fashion. Star jumps, running on the spot, jumping up and down as long as I am able to.

* And then, just before I arrive home, pinch my cheeks and spray myself in the face, under the arms and even in the crotch area with water from a spray bottle I kept in the car, stashed with my book, so not only would I look rosy-cheeked, I would also look a bit sweaty.

He was never really interested in where I went, but just the fact that I'd gone eased the tension a bit.

Towards the end of our twenty-six years of marriage, my self-loathing had become a creature that inhabited our relationship, an uninvited third party that neither of us could love. My husband started to spend more time with others, which was a relief for me because it meant I didn't have to spend as many hours pretending. We were both miserable with how our marriage had turned out.

His dream had been that we would grow old and content together like his parents and travel the world together as a fit, happy, adventurous couple. That I'd want to socialise with his new friends, who were all super-fit, healthy professional people. When I did meet them once socially, it seemed they weren't interested in me. Why would they be? I was overweight, unfit and I didn't know their in-jokes. I spent the evening trying to hide in a crowd of people, feeling very alone, although I did manage to have fun with my true and trusted friend – alcohol.

As the years passed we began to live as companions, leading separate lives with separate friends. We were pleasant with each other and were good parents to our growing children, but all the while we felt frustrated and misunderstood. We tried couples' therapy for a few months, but nothing would change as long as everyone, including me, thought I was still broken.

Eventually the third creature in our marriage forced my husband to see a therapist. He had two or three sessions, then told me he was leaving. So it was done and, if truth be told, we should have ended it sooner that we did.

It took me a number of years, and loads of therapy, to be thankful he was the one to leave, because I would never have had the courage to take that step myself. He was and still is a good man. He's a loving father to our two children and loving and supportive of his new partner (whom I really like, BTW).

Recently, I was explaining to a friend the parallels between therapy and The World's Largest Onion (TWLO weighs in at 8.5 kg – of course I had to look it up!). My analogy is that therapy is like peeling the layers of an onion, one by one, until there is only the most beautiful inner core left. For me the thick, outer layer of this whopper onion was peeled off when I started therapy. It wasn't so much peeling an onion as discovering that an onion actually existed and that I had a right to have a fucking onion in the first place.

Over the years, as each layer has been exposed and gently peeled away – or ripped away in a moment of epiphany – I have understood more about myself. I've been able to release resentments, forgive people for acts I thought unforgivable, see things with new eyes, discover positive attributes about myself, and start to understand more about my life journey.

Now we're close to the centre of Pammy's Prize Onion. We're at the final layers – the ones that represent the beliefs I've held onto most tightly in order to protect my frail inner core. The ones that must be addressed to uncover my essential essence.

And those layers of the onion seem to be the most difficult to peel away.

And now we're back to Supersized Me. I know perfectly well how to get fit and healthy, but knowing how to do something has not made me do it ... until now. Now I'm ready to try something, so I've started a six-month trauma yoga programme. Trauma-sensitive yoga is designed to create yoga poses that assist the release of tension so the body can learn new pathways to self-acceptance and peace. It took me nearly three years to build the confidence to join this class because the anxiety of relating to my body again was overwhelming. If I can radically accept my body (I'm not quite there yet but very close), then I'll have some freedom from self-persecution. With freedom comes choice. With choices I can move towards fully accepting myself and being free to improve my health.

Let's start to peel the final part of the little sucker and hope there isn't one more layer underneath.

Until recently I thought I knew its
name. It was hypervigilance and having
dysregulated thoughts. Then down came
a beam of light (and angels humming)
when a newish addition to my therapy
team asked me, 'What coping skills
do you use when you have this level
of anxiety?' Whaaat? I completely
dismissed her comment at first (yes, I did
apologise later because it was a pivotal
question that I hadn't recognised as
such). With all of my diagnoses over the
millions of hours I've been in therapy, the
word 'anxiety' had never been mentioned.
I thought it was every mental health issue
I had colliding together and was much
more complex than 'just' anxiety.

FFS, what's with the money guilt?

In about 2007 I declared out of the blue, in front of my husband and some mutual friends, that I was going to take long-service leave from my consulting gig to volunteer for a while. Since my husband was on a nice six-figure amount, and both of our children had graduated from their high school years (read no big fees anymore), I thought this was quite a reasonable request. It didn't go down well with him, but I think if I hadn't taken that break I would have had a complete mental breakdown because I was so very close to the edge without really knowing it.

While volunteering I did take on the occasional paid gig, but my heart was never in it. I couldn't understand why, oh why, when everyone else in the world seems to be able to enjoy making money, I would be dysfunctional in the area of finances. I certainly did and do enjoy being able to purchase what I need. Why, then, do I have such an aversion to making large amounts of money? Why do I always feel guilty, or ashamed of it?

I know my we-have-enough-money attitude was problematic in my marriage. My ex was a frugal man (he was of Scottish descent) and was always interested in making our money work smarter so we could make even more. He found it hard to comprehend, as others did, why I wouldn't use my consulting skills (which are considerable. Really! And acknowledging that is a proud and happy moment for me) to continue to make a very good income instead of 'wasting my talents' to volunteer. Why would I put time, effort and money into something that wouldn't benefit me directly?

My answer was 'Because I can.' The more I was encouraged to engage in professional work, the further I shifted away from it. The more I was misunderstood – including by me – the more determined I was to get even more involved in volunteer work.

This shift created a crack in the marriage that grew into a chasm too large to cross, and one I was not prepared to face.

In hindsight – and after some Schema Therapy – I concluded that I've never really valued money.

Having a father who boasted about how much he'd made from some of his fraudulent (read criminal) activities made me feel sad, but I couldn't work out why. I know I enjoyed the huge chocolate slabs he brought home from the pub on Friday nights, but the joy fell away somewhat when I found out his mate stole it from his work and Dad was one of his fell-off-the-back-of-the-truck gang.

I remember Dad proudly showing me about twenty high-end watches, still with the price tags on them. This was more than forty years ago, and some of the prices were over $2000. I was really scared that we'd get into serious trouble. I felt like I was a thief as well.

Many other items arrived home with Dad – diamond jewellery, pearls, gold coins etc. Part of his ritual was to show these precious things to my sister, Mum and me, let us touch them once, and make us watch him squirrel them away in the special hidey-hole he'd created in his wardrobe.

These items were not sold but were handed out as special gifts to family and friends – always accompanied by some sort of wink-wink statement so others actually knew that they were being given stolen goods. To this day I cannot work out why everyone seemed happy to receive them.

One birthday I was gifted a watch and an ugly diamond ring wrapped together (no box or anything fancy). I faked my gratitude and, not sure what else to do, hid my gifts so I wouldn't get caught with them.

The time Dad arrived home with two huge boxes of footy socks was even worse for me. He told my sister and me that we had to help him get rid of them by selling them at school! This was in the days of the VFL (Victorian Football League), before the AFL (Australian Football League) was invented, but these socks weren't even for VFL teams. They were in fact soccer socks, and back in the day that was not a game I knew anything about.

Dad told us we had to sell at least five pairs a week. I agreed (with a big sigh) because I knew disagreeing was not an option. I was about thirteen or fourteen years old and didn't have a big circle of friends, but I knew that somehow I had to sell those socks. I was embarrassed, ashamed, and probably not a very engaging salesperson. Every night of the first week Dad asked me how many pairs I'd sold and my answer was always none. He told me I had to try harder. In the second week I worked out that I just had to get rid of those bloody socks to get Dad off my back.

I still cringe when I remember how desperate I must have been. I'm not sure whether I wanted to please him, get his approval or simply stay out of trouble. At first I threw a pair or two into the bushes as I walked to school and gave the excuse that someone had stolen them from my bag. This resulted in Dad telling me how stupid and careless I was, so that strategy didn't work. Yet for a while I continued to dispose of the socks in this way. It's a bit funny now to think about how various people would have found a pair or two of extremely long, colourful socks in their garden. I did my best not to hide them in the same property each day.

But I had to bring money home, and the best idea I could

come up with at that time was to steal it. Initially I took it from Mum's purse, then funnily enough from Dad's change drawer. I would pay him for the stolen socks with money stolen from him. I thought that was a good idea. Until it wasn't. I was fearful that he would start to notice his money diminishing. It's quite ironic, on reflection: I was petrified of being punished for stealing money from the man who was wanting to make money from stolen socks! It was also quite sad that I was stealing money and lying, not knowing which was worse and knowing what a terrible person I was.

I don't remember who else I stole from – probably my sister and maybe my grandmother, and there were still more bloody socks to sell. My greatest cringeworthy act was stealing from my best friend's mum's purse – it still makes me feel sick in my gut. This lady was the one constant, kind person in my life and I stole from her. I'm welling up with tears as I write this, remembering the great shame of being caught with her money in my hand, and the true kindness she demonstrated by pretending she didn't see me.

She became one of my guardian angels. A week or so later she asked me to do some jobs around the house for pocket money. She never asked me why I was stealing from her, or why I needed the money, nor to my knowledge did she tell anyone else. And that is how I survived the Stolen Sock Saga.

PS: In recent years, many decades later, I spoke to my sister who was also conscripted to sell socks. Her memory of it is so different from mine. In her account, she sold a few then told Dad no one was interested in buying them. I was demeaning myself by lying and stealing, and Dad probably thought I was doing a great sales job! Such is the fate of the child who lives in fear of not being loved and is desperate to seek approval.

Some of my best friends reading this will be muttering, 'Pammy! Have you taken your meds today? You are all over the place!' And the scariest answer is, 'YES. I have taken those little fuckers and I feel even more unbalanced.'

FFS, I always assume it's my fault

Who would have thought I'd be ahead of Oprah in my thinking? It was about fifteen to twenty years ago that Oprah started her self-development journey and her 'Gratitude' concept. My self-proclaimed brilliant idea of *The Proud and Happy Book* was born the previous century – in 1993. Let me set the scene for you.

My daughter was in her first year of primary school when my son started his final kinder (pre-school, pre-prep) year. Both loved drawing, colouring and creating things, though since Rosie is nearly two years older than Larry, she had a better attention span and could sit still for longer.

My consulting career was starting to take off. I was away from home a few days a month, running conferences or workshops. Of course, I had to be the perfect mum, so school and kinder timetables took precedence over other appointments when I wasn't away on business. I thought I was doing an excellent balancing act: managing parenting, childcare and household duties while I was home, and making sure everything ran smoothly while I was away, with Backup Plans 1, 2 and 3 at the ready.

Larry attended Fairy Hills Kindergarten. There really is a suburb called Fairy Hills – how perfect for a child and his kindergarten. It was Larry's last year there and he really liked it – the kinder was situated in a lovely cul-de-sac, it was an excellent place for kids to explore and grow, and he had many friends from earlier years.

One day the teacher, Miss Sandy, asked to speak to me privately. Having had several casual chats with her previously, I was unprepared for what was to come.

She said she was questioning Larry's self-esteem. I was totally shocked. She told me Larry never wanted to take any of his paintings home. She'd asked him if he drew at home, and he'd said that he and his sister did lots of drawings at home and that Rosie was 'really good at drawing houses'. Miss Sandy had concluded that Larry didn't want to bring his artworks home because he thought they weren't good enough. She thought it was an issue that we should address at home since she had tried to encourage him to take his work home but he wasn't keen.

I left the meeting, sat in the car and did what I believed most mothers would do – I cried and cried (probably an early episode of bazooka tears – tears that come out parallel to the ground and can hit any target within ten metres).

Giving my children a sense of safety and the knowledge they were loved was one of my life's dreams. I'd never thought for a minute that my happy, outgoing boy who looked forward to going to every session could feel so bad about himself that he didn't want to bring his drawings home. Of course I thought it was all my fault, because I was working quite a bit and we had a casual nanny who picked up the kids once or twice a week when I needed help.

In any case, my automatic thought process at that time was *everything is my fault*, and I became a walking apology. My default thinking (de-fault) is *I'm da fault.* (Please, Dear Reader – this sentence makes sense in my head because I am using my very skilled and proficient rapper voice!)

Back to the bazooka-crying mother in the car outside Fairy Hills Kindergarten. What to do? How to fix this? (I didn't ask him then why he didn't want to bring his artwork home; that would have been way too logical! Haha.)

One of my greatest attributes is that I have a creative brain. I'm an ideas person! I can *do* ideas! An idea formed in my head – or, in the words of a three-year-old I know, explaining how she knew she wanted to be a vet when she grew up: my brain thought it up for me.

I would go straight to the newsagents. Do Not Pass Go and Do Not Collect $200.

I would buy a project book, some new pencils and some

fancy felt-tipped pens.

I would go home and create a title page that I would stick to the project book's front.

This book would be forever called *Larry's Proud and Happy Book*.

I was determined to help my little boy feel that he could be proud of all aspects of himself, his artwork included. Did I tell you that sometimes I have extreme reactions when a simple question might be the best solution? Annnyway ...

When I arrived to pick up Larry from kinder that afternoon I saw him happily running towards me. Of course he forgot his backpack, and as we went to collect it I asked, probably sheepishly, if he was bringing any paintings home today? The answer just reinforced my bazooka-tear theory. He said, 'No, Mummy.'

On the way home I asked heaps of questions about his day, as I always did – how was kinder? What did you do in outside play? What did you do inside today? What story did the teacher read? Was James there today? And so on, and on and on. I'm an extrovert, so this comes easily to me – my kids will agree that it hasn't quite stopped some thirty years later.

I had left my creative artistic project, the *Proud and Happy Book*, casually on the table, and when Larry sat down for a snack he asked what it was. I told him it was a very special book we could fill in each day when Rosie was at school. I went into full consulting mode (age-appropriate, of course), probably saying things such as: 'This will be a special way for you to remember what you loved about your kinder year. You could do a drawing and then tell me what it is about, and I'll write what it is, just like the teacher does on your paintings.' (Thank goodness he was four and had no idea that I was trying to 'save' him from potential years of therapy!)

Every day after kinder for the next couple of weeks we had a ritual. It comprised having a snack and a drink, getting out the *Proud and Happy Book*, Larry happily drawing in it, and me then being the scribe. Larry drew very creatively and just about everything had rocket blasters attached to it somewhere. He also wanted to learn some letters and got really skilful at writing his name.

In those weeks I didn't ask Larry to bring any artwork home. However, Miss Sandy did at times look over my way and shake her head, which meant that she'd asked Larry if he would take his paintings home and he hadn't wanted to. Big sigh!

One day I finally addressed the elephant in the room. I asked him (with my heart throbbing) if he could bring some of his art home from his kinder session that day. He stood still, sighed a little, and asked, 'Do I have to?'

Oh nooooo – alarm bells were screaming inside my head (not really, but I was a bit worried!).

I asked him the question I could have asked him weeks prior: 'Why don't you want to bring your art home, Lazza?'

His explanation rocked my world.

'Mummy, I do SO much drawing at home that I give to you. But Miss Sandy doesn't have any kids at home, so I give them to her to take home. Is that okay?'

Okay? Okay???!!! Of course it was okay!!!

This boy of mine didn't have a self-esteem issue. He had kindness dripping out of him. He knew I loved his drawings so much and that his teacher must be missing out because she had no children of her own, so he'd decided to gift his paintings to her to make her happy.

Oh, my golly gosh! Five Fat Sausages!

I asked him if I could draw in his *Proud and Happy Book* because my heart was so full with his kindness towards Miss Sandy. In his typical way, Larry didn't think this was a big thing. It was just factual to him.

We continued the tradition of the *Proud and Happy Book* that year, and he did start bringing some of his paintings home. After I'd told Miss Sandy what occurred, she told Laz that she couldn't fit another painting in her house and he could either give them to someone else or take them home.

He happily brought his paintings home after that. A few years later he admitted to me that he never really liked painting at kinder or the 'art stuff' because all he wanted to do was play outside!

Even though I still sometimes forget to ask questions that could save me an episode or two of bazooka tears, this *Proud and Happy Book* experience did encourage me to become more curious and, yep, I even learned to ask a few questions before jumping to the worst possible conclusions. As a result, I became a great, empathic listener.

Stay tuned for the next exciting episode of how the *Proud and Happy Book* concept lived on, morphed a few times, and ultimately became an essential part of life for quite a few people.

I must admit I am scared that the
roller-coaster may swing into action
at any time and that this peaceful feeling
of being okay may be short lived, but
hey – I am going to enjoy the respite
while it lasts.

FFS, it worked!

Around the time I cried bazooka tears outside my son's kindergarten and determined to be the best parent, wife, friend, consultant and volunteer I could possibly be, I'd taken a full-on dive into self-help books, including *Chicken Soup for the Soul* by Jack Canfield and Mark V. Hansen.

It's ironic that I wanted to read all these books in an attempt to improve myself for everyone else while neglecting the me inside. Sadly, at this time in my life I had not one self-worth bone in my body. I thought my worth was to be everything to everyone else – part of a profound, maladjusted belief that I wasn't and never would be enough. I wasn't even conscious of the notion that I should put my own oxygen mask on first. (Maladjusted belief systems are part of Schema Therapy. One thousand blessings – and 1000 camels perhaps – to Mr Jeffrey Young who discovered, researched and created this form of therapy in the mid-1990s.)

Dear Reader, my brain popped off again, so back to the story of 'I am fabulous for everyone else except me' days of my life.

I think it might have been when I was reading the very first edition of what was to become the *Chicken Soup for the Soul* empire that I happened upon a chapter titled 'All the Good Things'.

Hold that thought – me reading the above chapter.

Another little aside to this story is that, since 1993, over 250 editions of *Chicken Soup for the Soul* have been published. The two authors collected other people's stories, collated them, published them, and gained enormous money and fame from them. When doing a little research to find the chapter again, I browsed through all the titles. I'm sure there are many wonderful, inspirational stories in each book. However, I do ponder whether their hearts were still in it when the titles started to include: *Chicken Soup for the Soul: What I Learned from the Dog / What I Learned from Loving Our Dogs / My Very Good Dog* etc.

Cat lovers, don't worry. You also have your own series: *Chicken Soup for the Soul: What I Learned from my Cat / My Very Good Cat* etc.

Okay – I'm back on track now! Anyhooo …

'All the Good Things' is the touching story of a young nun, Sister Mary, and one of her maths classes during her first years of teaching. One day, in order to manage an unusual episode of bickering in her classroom, she told the students to write something they liked, admired or respected about each of the students in the class. She collated these compliments and hand-wrote them onto sheets of paper, which she then distributed so that every student had a sheet of positives about themselves. Peace returned to the classroom.

Some years later one of those students, Mark, died in Vietnam. Sister Mary was invited to the funeral by his mother, who said Mark had always spoken highly of her. At the wake after the funeral, a young soldier told her that he had been with Mark when he died. The soldier pulled out an old piece of folded paper with her handwriting on it and said that Mark had carried this everywhere he went and often read it when times in the field were tough. Other ex-classmates at the funeral also told Sister Mary how important their own sheet of paper had been to them and their lives.

Just like any moving and inspirational story, this one stayed with me. On reflection it was probably more significant than I thought at the time. I would love to have been a part of Sister Mary's class and had positive affirmations given to me during my formative school years. The fact that I was seriously bullied during high school – a problem that was never addressed – affected my entire life profoundly.

I have spent most of my life being a people pleaser and afraid of upsetting just about anyone! What Sister Mary gave these children, I think quite unwittingly, was a feeling of being valued and that they were enough.

The first time I referred to this story in a professional capacity was at a week-long conference a few years later. The company I was contracted to work with, a trade supply business, had acquired a smaller one. It had been what is coined in the business as 'a hostile takeover'. The CEO understood that the first year was critical for success, but in early discussions there was great resistance on both sides to addressing the many elephants in the room: cultural change, leadership, teamwork, respect and working towards a shared vision.

For the CEO, the board and the future of the company, my workshop with them was critical.

Prior to the five-day workshop, when I was introduced to the senior management team (a group of twelve men), the CEO stated that unless the team started to work towards the new joint vision, major resistors would be quickly identified and 'managed out' of the organisation – one of the buzz words for 'you're fired' in Organisational Change jargon back then. (Eeek, I have just had flashbacks to the early episodes of *The Apprentice* and He Who Must Not Be Named.)

The CEO also added that he expected all gripes and resistance to be sorted out at the workshop so they could find ways to move forward. If I recall correctly, 'We will work all this shit out!' were some of the words he used.

My stress and anxiety before the conference was off the

Richter Scale. My internal tremblings, if they'd been part of an earthquake, would have been big enough to divide Australia into two islands! I spent the entire weekend agonising: had I forgotten anything? Had I done enough deep research to ensure I had back-up plans for my back-up plans? Did I need another hundred inspirational quotes up my sleeve and ready to use if necessary?

It seemed that every moment was consumed with ticking off imaginary lists in my head. And of course I'd created lists that were ticked off then lost or deemed inadequate. When I expressed my doubts to my husband, he would say, 'Don't worry, you'll be fine.' This was supposed to be encouraging, but the voices in my head screamed, 'HOW DO YOU KNOW THAT?'

The conference started, and after four very long days and nights there was a sense of excitement for the future. Major breakthroughs had been made. New bonds had formed. Barriers had broken down. There'd been laughs, 'aha' moments and loads of personal sharing. They made plans and commitments to the team and were ready to lead, inspire, encourage and support each other. All, including the CEO, were thrilled with the results thus far.

The conference had exceeded my own or any other person's expectations, and at lunchtime of the second-to-last day I had one of my Pammy Brainwaves. It was exciting and would be a fabulous way to close the conference the next day. After a quick word with the CEO and gaining his agreement, I ran around like a headless chook to get that final afternoon session organised.

I made an announcement that as there is no such thing as certainty, the afternoon session was to be changed. I read them the story about Sister Mary. I told them about the *Proud and Happy Book* concept and how rarely we take the time to reflect on the positives in life. The task for the afternoon was to write at least one thing that they'd like to acknowledge each participant for. They could write as little or as much as they wanted, and were potentially giving a lasting gift to one of their new teammates.

I gave them the next four hours to work on their own and write their list. They could sign it or remain anonymous, and they were to return it to me prior to our final dinner together. I'd collate them so each person had an individualised list which I'd hand out after the review of the objectives and the closing speech by the CEO.

For the entire afternoon while they were doing this, I wrote my own thoughts about how each participant had added value to the conference. I was really excited with how well the participants had accepted the challenge, but also blissfully unaware of how this spontaneous activity – what I now call 'doing a Pammy' – would come back to bite me on the bum.

All the lists were returned to me. At the dinner some participants shared how much they enjoyed the exercise, and there were a few confessions about how hard it was to write a compliment and how their default thinking was always to look for flaws.

This final dinner was filled with laughter, enthusiastic conversations and all the feel-goods that bring joy into my life. When I finally left for my room at about 11pm I was exhausted. I had been trying to leave for about an hour but kept being asked questions or getting included in conversations.

As I started to sort the lists, I realised I hadn't accounted for all the steps that were necessary to get this ready for the 7.30am start the next morning. What I'd thought was a great idea kept me sitting on the floor until the wee hours, and as I finally unfolded myself to flop into bed I was starting to doubt whether this new brainwave was worth the effort.

Sleep didn't come easily as I was fearful I'd not wake up in time, and also that the entire conference could finish 'not with a bang, but a whimper' (thanks, T. S. Eliot).

I missed breakfast because I was so exhausted and a bit slow. By the time I entered the conference room, brightly saying, 'Good morning to all,' I had once again put on my shiny, happy, positive consulting face. Actually, this was not just my consulting face – it was the face I felt I had to show to everyone because I thought I had to be perfect.

The morning went as follows: 'blah blah', the CEO's amazing speech and thanks to all; 'blah blah', summary of objectives; 'blah blah', what each person had learned from the conference and what commitments they were making to move forward as a team member ... 'blah blah'. It may sound incredibly dismissive of all of the major outcomes of this conference but all I could focus on was the moment when I'd have to give out the envelopes.

At last, just prior to the official end of the workshop, I handed them out. I asked everyone to read the contents in silence. These were theirs to keep and I hoped it had been a rewarding exercise for them all.

Everything seemed to be in slow motion. I remember short intakes of air, looks across the room to catch someone's eye, nods of recognition, and a few tears being wiped. If I could have bottled the atmosphere in that conference room in those moments, I am sure we would have bottled world peace.

I started to close the workshop with some famous last words (an inspirational quote I was going to leave them with) when I was stopped by, 'Hang on a minute.' One of the most resistant, most cynical managers stood up and declared he'd like to say a few words.

When he first stood up I got myself ready for the normal 'blah blah, thanks', but NO – he said he had a major criticism about something that had really pissed him off! I felt as if I was either going to be sick or faint; my ears were ringing and my mind was screaming. Panicked thoughts raced through my head but somehow I nodded, put a smile on my face and said, 'Of course – I value your feedback.' My greatest fears were going to come true – I was about to be publicly shamed.

He said he had spoken to most of the other participants, and they agreed with him. (*Noooooooooooooooo! Please stop!*)

'Why didn't you put your name on the acknowledgement sheet? I had some really good shit I wanted to write to you.' He then said some very nice things that I didn't really hear and he started to clap. With that all the rest of 'my boys' stood up and gave me a huge round of applause! Of course I cried and cried, not moving except to look at each of them in the eye, and mouthing, 'Thank you.'

I was moved by their genuine kindness, but my overwhelming emotion at that time was massive relief that I hadn't messed up. I hadn't been publicly ridiculed. They asked for my email address, which I gave them, and each participant emailed me with their acknowledgements. Some emails were a few sentences; others were detailed and profound.

I thought then that maybe I should start a *Proud and Happy Book* of my own, but that was only a fleeting thought as I had the next conference to worry about: research to do, back-up plans upon back-up plans to create, and more inspirational quotes to find.

Over the next fifteen years, whenever I have organised a conference, worked with a team over a long period, spent time with my many coaching clients or needed to help friends who were going through difficult times, I have used some version of Sister Mary's story and the *Proud and Happy Book* concept, with a touch of Oprah's Gratitude Journals, and it has added huge value to many lives.

And yes, Dear Reader, nearly thirty years after creating the very first *Proud and Happy Book*, I have finally started my own!

Recently, in a regular chat with my book coach, Kathy, I was sharing about an interaction I had with a random stranger. After I told her what happened, I said, 'I love that part of me, the random part who acknowledges others.' Kathy stopped me mid-sentence and said, 'Since I first started to work with you fifteen months ago, this is the first time I have ever heard you even acknowledge something positive about yourself, let alone say, "I love this about myself".'

FFS, Amy Sherman-Palladino, you are NOT my friend

Do I know Amy Sherman-Palladino? Nope!

Does she know me? Even more unlikely!

So, you may well ask, why do I have such a dislike for this eight-syllabled person?

Have you heard the saying, 'If it sounds too good to be true, it probably is?' That's why.

Amy Sherman-Palladino, you are probably a lovely person. But you wrote the wholesome and appealing series *Gilmore Girls*. The mum in this series is quirky and funny, and her daughter, Rory, is a young teenager. As the series develops, Rory gains independence from her OTT mum while remaining lovingly tolerant of her way-out-there nature.

My daughter and I were dedicated to watching every episode of *GG* together for years. This was so long ago that if we were going to miss an episode we'd have to pre-programme the VHS so we could watch the tape later. If you don't know what a VHS is, you will never know the heart-breaking fury of untangling a mass of delicate black tape stuck in the machine that holds the one programme you must see.

Remember what my best mother–daughter relationship looked like, Dear Reader? Well, the Gilmore girls had exactly that. I truly believed we would ride lovingly into the sunset of our lives together.

Yes, it was a fantasy. Yes, I knew it was a tad unhealthy for both of us to be so intertwined and interconnected, but I longed for it just the same. The irony was that, in reality, our mother–daughter roles were so similar to those in *GG* – I was the quirky and at times embarrassing mum, and my daughter was the confident, successful and independent one. Sadly, this is where the similarities to the *GG* mother–daughter relationship endeth.

The *Gilmore Girls* fantasy was well and truly broken by the time my daughter was sixteen or seventeen. It has taken me decades to realise that the quirky, fun mum wasn't what my daughter thought a mother should be – especially not *her* mother.

So how did we get to that point? Even before I first conceived, I knew I needed to be my child's superhuman protector. I had to be everything my mother was not, and I made it very clear to my husband, prior to any discussions about marriage, that I was never going to smack my children, and I expected the same from my future partner. My yet-to-be-diagnosed complex childhood trauma and resulting PTSD drove every thought and action and triggered every protective nerve in my body. This tiny child of mine would feel safe, comforted and nurtured. They would know they were loved; they'd make their own choices and be believed, always; and they'd be strong and independent, and of course have the best mum ever!

My anxiety ramped up when our firstborn turned out to be a daughter. She was the most precious tiny gift, and I knew it was my life's purpose to protect her from hurt. What a bitch hindsight is. I was setting myself up for failure by minimising her father's role and being a maverick, a lone wolf, on a mission to repair the damaged child inside me.

My mother rushed to visit us as soon as Rosie arrived. She basked in the beauty of my gorgeous baby – never mind the enormous bruise on her bum! While she was cradling and cooing to my child, I said one of the cruellest things I think I have ever intentionally said in my life. I told my mother, in a soft, slow, deliberate and threatening tone, as she was having her very first cuddle of my precious bottom-first cherub, 'If you ever, ever smack or hurt my child in any way, you will never, ever, ever fucking hold or see my child again.' I emphasised and sneered out the f-word.

I still cringe when I think about my mother sitting there, hearing me spit out that unthinkable word, rocking her granddaughter for the first time. She nodded slowly and finally looked up, saying, 'She's just beautiful.'

If I'd only known then how she'd suffered, and what she had sacrificed for my sister and me, I would have thought Rosie was the luckiest child alive to have my mum as a nanna. In fact, she grandmothered them in the way I wished she'd mothered me. I will never forget the day I was invited to Mum's Probus Club to speak about one of the charities I was involved with at the time. She was so proud to introduce me and I was thrilled to be in the company of women who valued her. In one conversation I overheard, she was boasting about my children. She said something like, 'Oh, they are such wonderful children. Did you know I have never had to raise my hand to smack them?' She was talking to an audience of old-school smackers and they were ever so impressed.

But now we must head back to Season 4 or 5 of *Gilmore Girls*. By this point my daughter and I no longer watched the show together. In fact, we didn't spend much time together at all except when she wanted me to take her shopping, or when I was needed as a drop-off and pick-up service. I was always there for her convenience and desperately hoping still to win the Best Mum Ever contest.

My brain and my ever-unfolding mental health issues drove me to think I needed to be a different person, more like Lorelai, the loveable, approachable and always cheery

Gilmore mother – which also meant I didn't want to annoy or upset my daughter for fear of losing her. The fact that my mental health issues were not understood by my spouse, my children or even my friends led to some very dysfunctional enabling mum behaviours due to my desperation to recreate the *Gilmore Girls* dream.

One example of my desperate need to please was when Rosie was in her senior years of high school. She'd decided she wouldn't eat second-day bread for lunch. She would eat crackers and cheese, but in my mind crackers and cheese weren't good enough for my daughter, so to my shame and her amusement, I started popping down to the local bakery or the supermarket (to be known for ever more as the stupid-market) every morning to buy her favourite fresh bread rolls. (My son didn't come into this equation because he didn't care what was in his lunchbox and whether it was fresh or not – he was either too busy to eat or just found it too boring.)

I can't remember how long I fed this obsession, but it was at least two years of early-morning bread runs or the sickening knowledge that I had provided a second-class option of biscuits and cheese, even though Rosie liked a crackers-and-cheese lunch.

My daughter recently shared with me how much she loved my need to be the perfect mum. She seemed to delight in telling the story to her friends about getting fresh bread rolls collected and filled for her every day. I'm not sure she even knew how over-the-top my behaviour was.

Today Rosie's news comes to me mostly through other people: she seems to be kicking butt in the corporate world. She has a huge role in a huge company; she has a wide circle of friends and supporters; she is fiercely independent, intelligent, quick witted, resilient and future-focused. The fact that our relationship is not closer and that we are not in contact often does make my heart sad, sometimes to the point of torture. One of the hardest life lessons I've had to learn is to not define myself by the opinions of others, but until recently I hadn't applied this to my daughter.

One particularly dark day in the not-so-distant past I was lying in a foetal position on the floor, weeping about our situation. With great effort I rolled onto my back, looked beyond the ceiling and in a raspy voice, vocal cords damaged by endless wailing, pleaded with the Universe to tell me, 'What is my lesson?'

There was no answer, so I screamed, 'WHAT IS MY FUCKING LESSON?'

Imagine the sound of every angel and soul in the Universe – infinity plus one to be precise – laughing, giggling, chuckling, knee-slapping, all doubled over in laughter.

And the Universe, All-Wise, All-Knowing, responding calmly in a loving voice: 'Pammy – you cannot control anyone. They will make their own choices.'

The laughter was infectious and I smiled. I remembered that I gave life to a little girl. I got the joke and started to chuckle. As I struggled to sit up (just a little dramatic overplay for your pleasure, Dear Reader), I repeated over and over, 'I gave *her* life. I gave her her life. I gave Rosie HER life.' Laughing like a maniac, I kept going. 'I get it now. Her life. She can do what she wants with HER life! It doesn't matter if I don't like it – she is living HER life.' I broke into a hoedown song:

I have no control

I have no control

This gal Pammy

Has got NO control.

At that point I felt as if I was morphing from disciple to guru!

While my original dream was for us to have a super-close *GG* relationship and be BFFs, the more I tried to edge closer to her, the more she was magnetically repelled with equal force. Rosie is now strong and independent, as I always wanted and dreamed for her to be, but the irony is that I fucked up by trying so hard not to fuck up. Never wanting to, never believing that I could. And I did anyway.

Even though I think I can somehow control others' behaviours, in reality all I can control is how *I* react to situations. Not everything that happens to me needs to challenge my beliefs of right and wrong. I have to simply accept what's happening right now and adapt. Lightbulb moment.

It's very confronting that, for me, living my best life could mean that others might not like or respect my choices. Am I emotionally resilient enough to accept that? I live in fear of being judged – by my children, by my closest friends and by everyone else – but my greatest fear is being misunderstood.

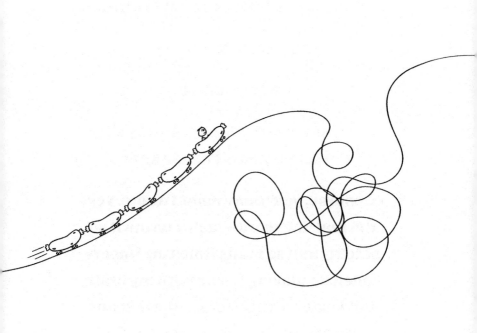

I don't want to write this. I don't want to write. I DO NOT WANT TO WRITE THIS!

Do. You. Get. It?????

I don't want to!

All I want to write is pages and pages of 'Fat, Fat, Fatty FAAAAAATTT'.

Of course, you know what I wrote. Yep, the real 'fat' word – fuck. I wrote it so quickly and so many times my fingers ended up playing tricks with my brain and I was writing things like fick and fuvk. My all-time favourite was focj.

FFS, those were troublesome years

Dear Reader, I want you to know how very difficult this next section was to edit. The draft was easy – I just vomited words out of my mind and manically typed them onto the page. But I hate the entire editing process, so I didn't re-read these chapters until recently. Kathy had tippy-toed around them for months. Finally, she gently suggested we start editing them, although she was worried that parts might be triggering for me.

We agreed that a lot of what I'd written beautifully (Kathy's word, not mine) might not align with the purpose of this book, which is to write my version of my life, the facts as I know them, without apportioning blame to myself or others. The truth I had exorcised onto the page was, in fact, distressing to read. It was brutally honest. Kathy questioned whether this honesty and self-deprecation would fit the book's purpose and suggested that editing would uncover hidden and empowering lessons – the breakdowns and breakthroughs.

I assured her I was fine with that approach and committed

to editing 'this stuff' by the end of the working week – it would be easy. Bahahaha. How wrong I was!

What I did instead: turned nine kilograms of tomatoes into sauce, washed every sheet, blanket and doona cover in my cupboards, cooked massive amounts of food to give away, and completed many, many other productive things.

I even managed to cook up a sinus infection that was so bad I was vomiting from the pain! I'm very talented at manifesting diversions.

Finally, with my heart in my throat, feeling nauseous, and wanting to avoid this particularly painful period of my life and the massive impact it had on myself and my family, I declared that I'd embark on the edit with kindness both to myself and to others.

Here we go.

The troublesome years, which involved me drinking way too much alcohol as a coping strategy, coincided with my children's inevitable teenage boundary-stretching dramas, some of which I have already alluded to.

Both Rosie and Larry had very busy lives. They were involved in hockey at club, school and occasionally rep or state level. Their training sessions and game times were often conflicting, there was always some sort of school event or extracurricular activity and each had a social life that required coordinating. I was the parent who needed to make sure everything was covered and scheduled, the perfect parent, but the good old 'fake it till you make it' philosophy was not working at all, and my feelings of massive unworthiness and internal torment seemed to quieten down only when I started to self-medicate with alcohol.

Drinking allowed me to escape the voices in my head. They were my constant companions, always highlighting how I was a disappointment and would never be enough of anything. But they calmed down with each sip, slurp or scull.

My alcohol consumption built up over a number of years. I never used to drink alone at home. Until I did. It was not every night. Until it was. I used to love going out with friends because my husband didn't drink – he'd made a conscious choice not to drink many years before, and I respected that – so I didn't have to be the responsible one.

When I drank I didn't care as deeply about doing what others wanted or expected me to do. I became a bit cheeky, even sassy. And this feeling was quite addictive. Or was it the alcohol? Maybe they were partners in crime.

The more I drank, the less I cared about other people's opinions of me. I knew I didn't like or respect myself, but it was a great escape, and somehow I felt powerful.

With each morning came regret, disgust and self-loathing because one of my worst nightmares was coming true – I was becoming just like my father! In my despair I began to feel like a fraud, questioning my own intellect.

After doing great work in the corporate world, being a highly paid consultant, assisting with the transformation of company cultures and individual lives, I gradually lost all my confidence and started to believe I couldn't continue to perform at such a high level. I became super-critical of myself and began to feel like a con artist; surely clients would find out my nasty secrets too – that their consultant of choice was as nutty as a fruit cake and a sneaky drinker?

In my Dysregulated Mind I knew I couldn't save myself. Even some of the people I loved most seemed to have given up on me because I couldn't function in a normal way anymore.

My brilliant solution was to make a difference somewhere – if I couldn't save myself, maybe I could help others feel significant. So, my career as a volunteer started!

The more miserable I was, the more involved in charity work I became. I created charities, then bigger charities, raised money for friends' charitable causes and volunteered my time to assist others in their own personal development. All in the pursuit of trying to find some sort of peace and purpose.

And my work did make a huge difference in the lives of others. I even won awards. And therein lies the paradox – even when I did make a difference, my brain would tell me it wasn't enough. No matter what I did, it was never enough.

Not only that but, as mentioned earlier, doing charity work instead of paid work became problematic for my husband. Even though he was on a very good wage, in his logical and rational thinking I could also be making money towards our retirement funds.

One could say (actually, it's my truth so I am saying it) that during those years I found any sort of conflict difficult to deal with and to process. I was so harsh on myself, trying to trick people into believing I wasn't insane, trying my best to meet their expectations, that when it became obvious that someone was disappointed or cross with me, my self-spiral into darkness accelerated.

Having been raised by a damaged and hyper-critical father and a mother who always needed to control the situation, I didn't relate well to heated discussions and differences of opinion. I retreated, feeling even more misunderstood and stupid. Often there would be an apology from the other person a few days later, which to their mind confirmed the end of the argument. But by that time I'd been left in a traumatised state, feeling cornered, stupid and powerless for hours or sometimes days. It always seemed too little, too late. I felt as if I'd been metaphorically beaten up, bruised and punished by an absence of kindness.

As I became more embroiled in this situation, I went out less and less often in public or to see friends. I did a lot of hiding and created lots of excuses, many of them fictional, so I could spend more and more time alone. After all, I knew I was the problem, and I couldn't fix me.

Biggest laugh! If only I'd known then what I know now. Isn't hindsight a giggle? A bitch? Totally useless? I suppose hindsight is good to reflect on the troubled years, to see them for what they were and forgive myself, because I *didn't* know then what I know now – and I only know it now thanks to 10,000 hours (my truth, remember, Dear Reader) in therapy.

The emperor has NO clothes.
This is the elephant in the room.
I am sitting here naked. Not literally
but figuratively. My soul is totally
exposed. I am raw, broken, and
completely stuck.

FFS, this is the REAL alcohol chapter

If you define alcoholic in medical terms, my drinking might fit. Could that be what I am? An alcoholic?

In my head I'm not, of course. I just drink regularly, in large quantities, and have been known to have zero alcohol-free days for months in a row.

I drink a lot of alcohol alone. A lot of alcohol. A lot.

When I am not alone I might have a few drinks before my guests arrive (in the evening only, of course). I will drink with them, and I will more than likely drink again after they leave.

I lie about the amount I drink, either to people's faces or by omission. But really, me? An alcoholic? I just won't have that.

If you were to timidly ask, 'Pammy, what would your therapist say?', I'd probably lie to you about that too. And I may have even lied once or many times to various therapists, probably to their faces and by the omission of my true relationship with alcohol.

I know it is not a laughing matter.

I don't want to be anything like my father: obese, with beer-stained clothes and smelling of alcohol.

I am not like that! Nothing like that. Sure, sometimes I don't have a shower for days. But that's because I have depression. Sure, I sit alone at home, drinking as if I could not give a fuck about my health or wellbeing. I know that drinking alcohol worsens depression. And, oops, I am in the morbidly obese weight category.

Maybe I do need to accept that I am a functioning alcoholic. (I cannot even admit to this stupid computer that I am an alcoholic – I have to make it sound better by adding 'functioning'. Truth be told, I would have preferred to lie a bit more and write 'high-functioning person with an excessive alcohol problem'. Of course, that sounds better!)

'What you resist, persists,' said someone at some time.

Fuckity fuck fuck fuck – what do I do now?

I'm haunted by a dream I had. I was so disoriented when I woke up that I believed the dream was true and I was on the brink of calling my psychiatrist to ask him to organise my entry into the Melbourne Clinic again.

In the dream my ex-husband was dying of liver cancer caused by alcohol abuse. But what if the dream was the Universe's way of telling me that I'm the one who's got liver cancer? And I'm the one who's been keeping secrets? My children would be so angry if I drank myself to death. Yet I'm scared to get a blood test. Because I don't want to confirm that I've damaged my liver. And because I'm scared to give up alcohol.

The fact is, when I drink I feel in control. I get this attitude of *Don't fucking tell me what to do.* Before my husband left I'd sit up on my own drinking Scotch and Diet Coke. Because I knew I had to lie next to this man and I wanted to be so drunk that if he touched my body I could cope.

Oh, that's a big, long silence.

So now we're getting to the nitty gritty of this. I was unhappy in my marriage for a very long time before it ended. I drank to hide the fact that I didn't want to be there. Actually, I didn't want to be anywhere. I wanted to see if I could blink and disappear. So I drank. And I hid the fact that I drank.

You might be able to tell that this whole dream analysis stuff has really scared me but I don't want to address it and admit it. Do I have liver cancer? Am I dying? I'm too scared to contemplate that, too scared to go to the doctor to get the blood test. And then my brain says, *Well, if I've already got liver cancer it doesn't matter if I drink.*

Very very very long silence.

So, if you define alcoholic in medical terms, maybe that is what I am. But most of the time I don't drink a lot of alcohol alone. I only drink to excess if I've been triggered – by things that hurt me, by things that confuse me and sometimes by things that bring me great joy. Such is the beauty of my complex mental health diagnosis – everything is fair game. Yes, even the happiest times of my life can sometimes send me spiralling into the depths of doom and darkness. But unlike my dad, alcohol no longer has complete hold over me.

Recovery is scary. I have struggled for a long time, and I have lost who I am and my sense of independence. My identity became my diagnoses. The thought of recovery, to me at least, was the unknown. Who was I on the other side of this struggle? Who was I without my depression? After many years of gradually having my identity chipped away, I had lost myself.

Recovery means leaving the familiar illness and 'life as you know it now' behind, venturing into a world of wellness that is uncertain and unfamiliar. You might feel anxious, irritable, and want to retreat back to your old depressed self. You don't know what to expect, especially if you've had trouble remembering what you were like before the depression began.

FFS, Kathy Derrick! That wasn't on my list

I don't even know how to start this chapter. I haven't written anything for ages. I've stalled for many reasons – some valid, some made up, some convenient. (Notice, Dear Reader, how this process of self-acceptance really is a roller-coaster of a ride.)

But I need to focus. Last week in our coaching session I bazooka-ed my book coach, Kathy, with an overwhelming list of issues that just blurted out of my mouth: project after project that I'd committed to, opportunities I couldn't ignore, feelings of betrayal, disappointments, new ways to move forward, acceptance, excitement, a run-down of my therapy sessions, enormous breakthroughs – everything that had happened in the last seven days and what was ahead for the next seven.

I also told her that there were so many new things I wanted to write about but that I felt too paralysed to write even a bullet-pointed list.

She was kind, understanding and wanted to help. I told her I had space to write in the next week, so together we worked on a list. I'll repeat it here just in case I lose the piece of paper I wrote them on.

* Recovery is Possible

* Being Psychic

* Betrayals and Forgiveness

* Emotional Transformation

* Inspiring Others

* Creating, Creating, Creating

* How Exhausting I Seem to Others at Times

* Feeling Alive Instead of Dead Inside and even more surprising - Having a Groin Tingle Again!

I also felt brave enough to request that she call me to account. I know, right? What a turnaround for someone who was paralysed by overwhelm a few short minutes ago, and who went into a foetal position a couple of weeks ago when Kathy asked me to 'just watch the time count down from sixty seconds to zero'. No writing, nothing, just watch the clock tick down.

I asked her to give me a deadline within seven days to write 1500 words on a topic from my list that she might be interested in reading. Even if it never made it into the book, at least it would be out of my head!

AND, Kathy – here is my dilemma – you did just as I requested. You asked me to submit a piece by the Sunday before our next coaching session, and the topic: What Does Love Mean to Me?

I didn't even think it was on my list! The one topic I want to avoid at all costs. Giving love to others is so, so easy. Giving any back to myself – what a horrendous thought!

I had a great excuse for not writing from Monday night to Wednesday morning. One of my besties came and stayed with me for a few days and we spent it doing not much: laughing, talking crap, having Deep&Meaningfuls, exploring life and the current world crises.

After she left mid-morning Wednesday I promptly jumped back into bed, intending to do a voice recording to start my thinking process. Well, that didn't work, so I got up and did a load of laundry for a friend. Not only did I wash everything, I also ironed her three-year-old's flannelette pyjamas, tee-shirts, shorts, even undies! I then spent hours reading resources about early childhood autism in case my friend needed them (she hasn't asked me to do this, of course), and checked the year-end balance of my superannuation account to get really depressed about how much I have lost in the last six months.

But wait, there's more. I completely rewrote a résumé that I'd done for a friend who said she needed it, when in fact I cared more about getting it to her than she did about receiving it. I changed the bedlinen and started to organise my receipts for my tax returns, which we all know I won't do until at least October. I looked at overseas airfares that I can't afford, contacted some people I know in India because a friend in England wants a recommendation for a tailor for a trip there in October, even cooked my dinner at 3.30pm because basically I had some free time. I then decided to search Spotify for the 'best ever writing music', and now I am listening to music I have no idea if I even like but at least I am writing gibber.

Getting all of this down has given me 1050 words with no problems. (Please don't count them, Dear Reader, there is more to this story – and besides, most of them will have been edited away.)

Nearly three days later and I think I've now graduated to Dr Pammy Wood, with a PhD for Active Avoidance & Procrastination – Double Dissertations.

But I have done some research and asked other people, 'What does love mean to you?'

Did I find any solace in their answers? No, they were all beautiful and seemingly unachievable fantasies. (Oh, Negative Nelly – hello, you're here too. I'll have to tell you to piss off soon.)

Damn! THIS IS REALLY HARD!

You already know that I was a sad and lonely girl with a dysfunctional upbringing, desperate to feel some sort of connection with people.

As an adult I can look back on those times and understand that my parents showed love to us within their limited capacity. I don't believe they had any loving family role models to base their parenting on, so how could they be anything else?

Mum showed her love by working tirelessly, providing food, bringing in a steady income, doing all the household chores on her own until we were able to assist, even making her own clothes so that she could save money to pay for our needs. We never missed a meal (except for the times I was punished and wasn't allowed to leave my room for dinner).

Dad, on the other hand, could be surprisingly nice to us, and it was these nano-seconds that I craved. He would bring home the odd block of chocolate for us to share, he would wink occasionally – small scraps of kindness that I'd yearn for in the decades to come.

If we're talking about love, we also need to talk about sex. You know a little about what my Pop did to me and how that made me a naughty girl – so it'll come as no surprise that Mum never told me anything about sex, about healthy boundaries, about consent, or that sex could be a wonderfully delicious and positive journey.

She couldn't tell me because she knew nothing about it herself. Remember, she was a virgin when she married, my dad called her frigid on their wedding night, and I have horrible childhood memories of being in the room right next to theirs and overhearing Mum begging Dad to stop. Combine this with a few other unwanted sexual experiences and confusing events during my pre-teen years and I was one very scared and unprepared girl when I started to have some groin tingles about boys in Form 3.

One day around this time Dad tossed a book into my bedroom called *The Little Red School Book* – in his words, to have a look through. He thought he was being clever and told me not to tell anyone, especially not my mother. He said it was banned in Queensland so must be good. Thanks to Dr Google, I later found out it had been banned by multiple countries around the world for being pornographic, and when the Australian censors finally developed the rating system, they wanted to rate it R: over 18 only.

What was in it was so out of context for me at that age. Pages and pages of different sexual positions, how to masturbate, how to use things to masturbate with, how to give hand jobs and head jobs. This information threw me to a whole new level of terror and intimidation because I knew, at some level, that if I did any of these things, I'd be a very bad girl.

Fast forward (oh, how I love the speed those two words provide) through embarrassing dates, underwhelming fumbled attempts to please boyfriends and being raped at nineteen, until finally, at age twenty-five, I met my future husband. He was my knight on a white horse, an attractive and kind man and he loved me. I also felt loved and accepted by his parents and their friends – I'd found a place I could belong. I knew what I had to do. If I could make their son happy, I would be loved in return – I'd found what love meant and the fairy tale could continue.

When my children were born I felt love at a whole new level. I never thought I could love anyone so much. I also knew what a dreadful world it was out there, so now love equalled protecting them at all costs from being abused or preyed upon. And if I protected them enough, surely they would love me forever?

It is no surprise that this sort of love-seeking was exhausting and unsustainable, and eventually left me feeling empty, hollow and unlovable.

In 2002 I completed a programme called The Landmark Forum. This gave me a new perspective on my life. I discovered I'd created the whole concept of being unlovable to make sense of a dysfunctional family dynamic. After realising this I was able to forgive my grandfather, because he must have been a very damaged man to take advantage of his young granddaughter. And I was able to forgive my mum for being unable to protect me. Later, I got to hear her anguish about her inability to keep me safe and how she'd hoped I had gotten over it because I seemed so happy. We began to build a new relationship, one based on honesty where we shared our own experiences. It became rich and loving, the mother–daughter relationship I'd dreamed of. I also reached out to my estranged sister and we too started to build a relationship that we both now treasure. Many more positive things happened, including my husband doing the course, and for a short time we felt more connected than ever before. I felt seen, I felt loved and appreciated for who I was. I felt complete.

Unfortunately, the transformation that was blossoming between my husband and me started to diminish when he decided he'd got enough from Landmark and didn't need to do any more. He went back to his life, his work, being a supportive father and husband, while I continued to learn and to coach and mentor others. I was great at this. I loved the deep connections. I loved the breakthroughs I was having and the potential of what and who I could be.

All this took my attention away from my family, and especially from my husband. I started to prioritise my time for others ahead of what my family expected from me. Recently my daughter confessed how hurt she was at this time. She felt as if I was no longer there for her, that I was always on the phone to others, and said it significantly impacted her life. When she shared this it was a total revelation to me, because our memories differ so much.

My memory includes trips to hockey training twice a week as well as to weekend and night games, driving her to and from high school, attending every home game of her beloved AFL team with her, having her friends over both at our Melbourne home and our holiday home, getting fresh bread rolls every morning for her lunch and trying desperately to be the best version of a mother that I could be. Wasn't this love? But in her mind it was black and white: I hadn't been available to her.

As the years have passed I have become very clear about what love means to me. It means making a connection with others and maybe making their day a little brighter. It can be as complex as creating a charity to bring life-changing initiatives to a village in Uganda, or as simple as a smile or a nod of acknowledgement. But what about the most vital aspect of love, I hear you ask? If you can't love and respect yourself, Pammy, you are really missing the whole point.

So, yes, I can finally acknowledge that there are things about me that I love. I have a kind heart – maybe too kind, some might say; I'm joyous and I love to spread that joy; I make connections with people from all walks of life; I have diverse and loving friends; I love being resilient; I love my compassion and forgiveness, my dark humour, my connectedness and curiosity; I embrace my neuro-diversity and accept that I am not for everyone. For my highest good and greatest joy and that of the lives I touch, I am going to take a little bow and say, 'Well done, Pammy.'

The beauty of all of this soul-searching, Dearest Kathy and

Readers, even though it is exhausting at times, is that now when I am in a very dark place I fully believe I will see that chink of light again. Just like hearing my children laughing spontaneously when I was so convinced I didn't belong in the world.

And now, Dear Reader, if you are brave enough, turn the page and immerse yourself in Part Two to receive more of my gift delivered straight to your eyes.

What gift, you may well ask? It's the gift that keeps on giving! Is it kindness? Nope. What about laughter? Double nope. Well, what the bleep is it, then?

It's the unexpected gift of the roller-coaster ride that is my Mental Health Journey.

PART TWO

Now that I'm here, what the fuck do I do next?

FFS, who the hell is Bob? (and other sexy disasters)

Dear Reader, the ten-year anniversary of being made redundant from my twenty-six-year marriage is approaching.

Apart from during the early stages of grief, anger, rage, betrayal, disbelief and shame that it was probably all my fault, I have not really missed being married or being in a relationship. What emerged, after the initial shock of my ex's self-actualisation needs (he said he was a good person and deserved to be happier than he was) and his subsequent exit from the marriage, was a great sense of freedom. By leaving, he freed me from all the shoulds and should nots I had believed about what it meant to be his wife. In his head he'd already moved on, and in a short space of time he had a new partner (have I mentioned that I still really like her?). And I too have certainly enjoyed the freedom to choose what I do, and how and when I do it.

My first post-marriage foray into sexual exploration came after having a discussion with a lovely younger friend. It was about a year after my uncoupling, and I told her I wasn't missing sex at all. Her opinion was that I could sex myself up a bit. She asked if I had a BOB. I said, 'A what?'

'A BOB!' she said. 'A battery-operated buddy!'

I exclaimed, 'Ew – nooooooooooo!'

We both laughed until she insisted that, right then and there, she was going to drive me to a sex shop! I cringed, thinking this was going to end very badly. But by the time we were in the car I was giggling like a naughty girl.

Off we drove to the closest 'SexyLand', or some equally abhorrently named premises. To my horror there were already cars parked outside. WTF – at two o'clock in the afternoon? I clearly knew nothing about the sex industry.

She dragged me inside and an absolutely gorgeous, high-pitched male voice excitedly squealed, 'Well, hello, darlings! What can I help you with today?'

My girlfriend said something like, 'I am bringing my remedial masturbating friend in to have a look around.'

We laughed, though mine was sort of a pathetic whimper, and we started to look at the unfathomable things on display. She knew quite a few names for them and, after looking at some I knew I would never use, she decided I needed a bullet! Oh, good choice, all my sexually aware readers might think. Although 'Whaaaaat?' is more likely to be in the minds of readers like me.

To the uninitiated, a bullet is a small, index-finger-shaped BOB. This is where our lovely shop assistant became involved. He asked a few questions and pointed us to a selection of appropriate BOBs. My friend was so excited when she saw the ones with diamantes on them. She turned to our sales assistant and said, 'What about one like this?' He said, 'You're welcome to try it, if you like.'

I instantly exclaimed, 'Ohhh, nooo!' But he laughed and said, 'No, silly. You try it on the tip of your nose because that's your most sensitive part, except for your clit.' By now my face was aglow with embarrassment and I just wanted to run out of the shop. But he seemed oblivious to this and took it out of the packet, put some batteries in and showed me how to turn it on. It had all sorts of vibration levels – haha, I wonder how many of you are cringing right now, just as I was then.

I dutifully took this bedazzled purple bullet and put it on the tip of my nose. There was an instant zap through my entire body and I must have exclaimed something like 'whoa' because he said, 'Get that one, darling!'

My friend purchased the pink bejewelled one and I chose the matching purple one, and we left the shop.

Fast forward five years to the time I found it in my undies drawer, unused. I looked at it and thought, *Maybe I should give BOB a spin*, only to find that the batteries had eroded and sort of exploded inside. I remembered the salesperson's squeal of delight when he heard I was a remedial masturbator buying my first BOB, and imagined his sad little face if he ever found out that this under-used potential fountain of joy had received such an undignified ending. I gave up on receiving pleasure and, not sure I'd want it ever again, unceremoniously dumped BOB into the bin.

Maybe five years after being made redundant, and in a moment of madness, I created a big, hairy, audacious goal to go on at least one date that year. It seemed achievable – surely! I signed up to eHarmony for six months. This gave the biggest discount, and enough time to go on my one date. (Although I didn't check the policy about auto-renewing – another Pammy Mistake.)

I may or may not have become a little bit obsessed with checking the dating app inbox once or forty times a day. I thought that the nearly honest profile of myself – kind, committed to making a difference and, if someone could look beyond my Rubenesque figure, a deep, compassionate, interesting and at times delightful companion – would attract at least some genuine interest. I didn't include the bits about self-loathing, being petrified of dating, or that I wasn't really ready to be in any sort of a relationship except with a eunuch or someone with erectile dysfunction, so I was surprised when no one contacted me.

I decided, if it's to be, it's up to me: I would make the first approach. I read profiles of men who described themselves as honest, who were great listeners, spiritual not religious, and genuinely interested in meeting a 'real woman'. I bravely contacted some of these men (who, by the way, did not resemble Adonis).

Again, why was I surprised when they sent a reply thanking me for my contact but saying they didn't think we would be compatible? I decided it must be my Rubenesque description that made these men want to vomit, so suggested in response that they update their profile and either remove the honest bit and/or include that anyone who was not slim, attractive, a sex fiend or a younger woman need not apply.

The only contact I did receive in the first three months was a long message from a lovely-looking man (judging by his photo). His profile stated that he was an engineer and, surprise, surprise, he just happened to be living overseas *and* wanted my personal email address or phone number because his profile had just been hacked.

The long message this man wrote was extremely complimentary and he seemed interested to find out more about me. Luckily, I had researched how to avoid being scammed on dating sites and am such a sceptic that I didn't fall for this Internet Dating for Dummies trick – no, no!

When I replied that I didn't feel comfortable emailing him

directly and could we continue corresponding through the eHarmony site, his entire profile disappeared from the site. Poof – vanished into cyberspace. I was sure I had escaped a bullet – and definitely not one of the BOB variety.

Imagine my surprise when I received the exact same message, with the exact same photo of this man, who had only changed his profile name and location? My first thought was *What a dick!* A dick with a dick – how appropriate. So, I responded accordingly. I may or may not have told him what a dick he was, along with some other juicy words, and how he'd already contacted me through this site, and that if he was trying to scam potential lovers the least he could do was write a list of who he'd already tried to scam so as not to contact them again. I also suggested that maybe he should give up his day-job of cyberstalker, or at the minimum learn more about algorithms, and I may have suggested that he fuck off!

I reported this faker to eHarmony with all the evidence I'd gathered, thinking Crime Scenes Investigator shows would surely want to recruit me. I thought I might get some sort of response from the company who insisted they cared so much about their members. In my imagination they would even send a gift basket and offer me a life membership for being so helpful. Surprise, surprise, I received none of this – not even a response.

Did I immediately cancel my subscription? 'That would

be the obvious thing to do,' I hear you say. Some of you might even be screaming at me, 'Of course you should!' Sadly, me being me, I just slithered off the app and did what all good ostriches do – buried the problem by total avoidance.

Maybe (who will ever know) my thinking was that if I logged out for a couple of months, I could rejoin after my six-month subscription ran out and maybe still get that one date. Oops, remember what I suggested earlier – it seemed I'd already paid in full for a further six months, this time with no introductory discount. (*Arrrrgh,* you scream, *will she ever learn?*) But hiding has been my go-to for personal challenges for many years. Of course I'll never admit this to anyone – well, except to the few of you still reading, who are either bored with your own life or waiting hopefully to see if there is a happy ending to come from this truly painful experience.

Six years down the track I can probably state with confidence that I am not physically repulsive, despite my earlier beliefs, even though I also know I'm not the recommended weight for my height. I continue to battle with body image issues – but I also remind myself I'm a loving and kind person who has the capacity to make light of most moments. I am seriously loved by some people and have huge, pelvic-floor-challenging laughs with them, and I seek to make a positive difference in most aspects of life. I'm not sure that telling the engineer from eHarmony to fuck off was so positive, but hey,

I'm human.

I digressed – sorry.

Back to the eHarmony story. December arrived. Was I going to have that one date and tick off a random and costly goal that I now wasn't sure I wanted? Of course I was!

I logged back in and was contacted by a man called Steve. He lived at least three hours' drive from my home, so I thought this was quite safe. Risk-taker me eventually spoke to him on the phone – yes, I did – and we exchanged a few texts. This could be a potential love story for eHarmony to publish on their website. But I was running out of time to have that one date, so I finally accepted an invitation to meet him during the week before Christmas. Hallelujah – another giant step for humanity. To this day I'll never understand why I subconsciously sabotaged this meeting and nearly ended up in hospital with major burns.

As he would have to drive for a few hours to meet me, he got to choose the place. I had a new outfit for our date, and I was going to make a silk purse from a sow's ear (if your grandparents aren't still going strong you might have to Google this saying).

I still don't know why I decided it was a good idea to degrease my rangehood that morning. (Seriously, no idea!) I had never considered doing this in all the years I'd been living in my post-divorce home, and when I looked up I could tell the previous owners hadn't done it either. It was disgusting!

I wasn't meeting my date until 1pm, so I had all the time in the world to attend to this vital task.

In retrospect, I should have read and paid attention to the large red writing on the side of the degreaser can.

As I was spraying the stuff onto the rangehood surface I became aware that it was running down my arm. A random question popped up: *Should I have worn gloves?* I looked at my arm and saw that my skin had started to bubble where the degreaser had made contact with it. I didn't think that was very good, so I ran cold water on my arm. And then the pain hit. In shock, I went next door and asked my neighbour what she thought I should do, only to find myself immediately bundled into her car and driven straight to my doctor's clinic.

While the doctors were debating whether I needed to go to a burns unit, I was trying to manoeuvre my arm under the cold water tap of a tiny hand basin. It took some physical origami to ensure the cold water reached the burn, which was becoming increasingly painful.

In all of this I managed to contact my date and tell him I couldn't meet him at the agreed destination, but if he was still wanting to catch up maybe he could come to my doctor's suburb and we could meet after I'd had treatment on my arm.

Surprisingly, he agreed, and I told him I would call him when I left the doctors. Did I tell the doctors (who were all now in attendance since the clinic had closed, and all offering differing opinions on how to treat my chemical burns) that I needed to get fixed so I could go on my first date in five fatting years? Of course I did, including asking these concerned doctors if I should go home and change into a nice outfit or just go as I was.

The doctors finally agreed I should have my arm wrapped in a film that not only drew heat away from the burn but would also keep it sanitised. This sounded all very good to me as I needed to get to that date – there were only ten days left before the end of the year, after all. The doctors hadn't solved my problem about what I should wear, but a receptionist did ask me to tell her how the date went!

I contacted Steve, thanking him for being so patient and warning him that I was not dressed to impress but would still like to meet him. We agreed on a Japanese restaurant since he'd apparently lived in Japan at one stage.

From his profile photo and our conversations, my image of him was a 6ft 4in big bear of a man who would undoubtedly give great cuddles. I also thought this could be good for both of us as we could go on a health kick (maybe Weight Watchers) together. Reality is always stranger than fiction. I watched Steve waddle towards me, at most 5ft 4in and as wide as he was short. My immediate thought was, *This could work – we could both seriously lose weight together*, as I was still under the impression that he was a nice man.

Oh, how wrong could I be?

I admit I was very overweight, but I did not have any issues with my joints – and I did not waddle. As Steve headed for the restaurant, he informed me that his knees and/or ankles could give out at any moment. I continued to remind myself over and over that I shouldn't make any hasty judgments since I was not exactly a rose myself. I was also nearly delusional because of the searing pain throbbing in my newly melted arm.

When we were seated at our table Steve presented me with a small gift. Oh, this is a nice start, you might think. But before I could open it he told me it was Lindor chocolates that had cost a lot. Well, now I didn't feel a need to open the present since I knew what was inside. Then he asked where *his* present was. I stared at him, gobsmacked. Is there some first-date-in-a-thousand-years etiquette that determines you exchange gifts? Maybe, since it was close to Christmas, I should have thought to bring this unknown man a gift, but I had not.

I tried to cover up my obvious etiquette fail by offering to pay for the meal. Oh, what a great guilt-trip strategy! His retort, that there was no way in the world he would ever let a woman pay for his meal, gave me another glimpse into the soul of this man I had been so desperate to date.

Steve then got out his phone and started to show me photos of his glamorous house, which he no longer lived in due to a friend owing him money. There were a whole lot of words about how he was trying to serve this man a summons for debt collection. Apparently, he had it all planned. He gleefully informed me that the man had a brother who was due to die from cancer any day soon, and this would be the perfect timing to serve him with the papers. What a way to convince a first date of your charming character, Steve.

Why did I not run out of the restaurant screaming? You may well ask.

But wait, it got worse.

He clicked his fingers to the waitress and said, 'Hey, China', to get her attention. In a Japanese restaurant, please note.

Then he told me his son was a great disappointment because he was a WWOOFer. I had no idea what this term meant, and he explained it stood for Willing Workers On Organic Farms. I thought this was quite a noble intention but was drowned out by Steve's insistence that his son was a waste of space.

I don't remember much about the rest of the torturous date except that I have never eaten so quickly in my life. At last it was time to leave. He insisted on paying – well, I had listened to his drivel and whinging so I thought that was fair – and we exited the restaurant.

As if what I'd been through wasn't enough, he asked when we could catch up again. He seemed puzzled then angry when I kindly told him I didn't think another meeting would be of benefit to either of us. His final comments were something like, 'Enjoy your chocolates and I'll enjoy my invisible present.'

Did I tell him what a self-righteous wanker he was? Of course not – but I really wish I had. At least the date finally made me cancel the fund-sucking dating app that had promised so much and delivered so little. And I was gifted a great story to add to the growing tales of Pammy's Roller-Coaster World.

The years went on uneventfully. I had no great need for romance or any partnership apart from contact with my regular friends. I even started to explore the concept of asexuality. Maybe this was what I'd transformed into – or maybe it was who I'd always been, even before it was a thing! I considered whether I might be a BAV (Born Again Virgin). And my care factor was zero.

Fast forward a few years (I love these fast forwards, very roller-coastery of me) to a bizarre WhatsApp conversation in January 2021.

I received a message from a man I'll call Roman – I won't use his real name because he's an international figure in the United Nations, from Italy. Thankfully, there are many Italian UN representatives so it would be very difficult to find out who he is.

Roman's cover story for contacting me was that we'd met in Uganda in 2018 and he was wondering how my charity was progressing. He indicated that I might not remember him. I replied that indeed he was correct: I didn't remember him. But I gave him the details of the charity website so he could look up how it was progressing, as well as our Facebook group details. Roman wrote back that he didn't use Facebook, and I thought that was the end of the conversation.

A couple of weeks went by and Roman sent me a photo of my charity business card that I'd apparently given him in 2018. I wasn't sure how he'd got this because I don't give those out freely, especially in Africa.

This time when I replied, I admitted we could have met but the details were vague. He sent me a photo of himself, and I did remember speaking to him prior to a flight out of Uganda in 2018. He said he'd been on a United Nations mission. Now I felt seriously bad as I'd tried to fob him off as an 'unknown'. Your guard goes up when you work in Africa – many people want to befriend you, all with their own agenda and often involving monetary assistance.

Roman and I exchanged some messages about what we'd been doing over the last two years. Then he asked if he could Facetime me. I didn't think that would be much of an issue so said yes. How wrong could one be?

He greeted me on our initial Facetime by saying something

like, 'Oh, baby, it's so lovely to see you.' Alarm bells started ringing, but did I end the call? Of course not, Dear Reader, and the conversation went completely downhill from there.

Roman must have thought he was being super sexy. He told me he was so excited to see my face and that all he wanted to do was to kiss and hug me. I was seriously creeped out but tried to laugh it off.

He pursed his lips, reminding me of a puffer fish, and started making kissing motions towards the camera on his phone. I was not only repulsed but felt quite violated. Did I leave the call? Of course not – do you not know me by now? I laughed and tried to remain kind. I did tell him, though, that I wasn't going to send him any kisses over the phone.

Then it got really creepy. He asked me to show him more than my face – to turn the phone down towards my tummy. As if this is a feature I'd highlight even in good times, and that night I had on one of my least attractive tops with no bra – ew! I said no, I wouldn't do that, but he kept on begging. Did I end the call? Well, you already know the answer. I don't know WTF I was thinking. Why didn't I stop talking, hang up immediately and block his number? Please, Dear Reader, there is a lesson in here for you!

Finally, I politely told Roman I was very uncomfortable with everything that was happening and I had to go. He said he'd ring me the next night and sent me a whole lot of flower, heart and kissing emojis.

I'd thought he was a nice humanitarian but now I wondered if he'd just found my card lying around somewhere. I rang my friend of the Swearing Burkes fame and told her the story. We had a few big laughs and she said, in all seriousness, 'Maybe you need to be kind to him in case he has early Alzheimer's, or perhaps he's just had a stroke – that could be why he's saying those things.'

I laughed so hard it hurt my throat, then said to her, 'Of course, the only men who could possibly find me interesting are those with Alzheimer's or who've had a stroke!'

My friend totally tried to backpedal, saying that wasn't what she meant, but I continued to pretend to feel devastated that she would think I was attractive only to senile or brain-damaged men. Oh, how we both laughed for a very long time.

I had to ring her back about an hour later and tell her I'd found another category of men who found me disturbingly attractive.

After our huge laugh attack I'd gone out, and as I drove around my local corner I saw a youngish woman with long hair slumped on the opposite kerb and a man watching her. I stopped my car and inquired if they needed any help. The gorgeous *she* turned around and became a gorgeous *he* (or perhaps a gorgeous *they*). They were clearly drunk (or high) and were very thankful I'd stopped my car to ask if they were okay. This young person's friend was just standing there, presumably being the responsible one.

So, this very, very drunk, handsome young person with a huge smile came across the road and told me I was gorgeous. I told them they reminded me of my son in his younger years. My son was everyone's best friend when he was drunk and he grew into a magnificent man. This young person asked if they could kiss me! So I said, 'Sure, on my cheek'. They planted a big kiss on my cheek, and when they stepped back they said, 'If I was really, really old, I'd find you really attractive.' BAHAHAHAHA.

I told them that their mum would want me to tell them they really should zipper up their pants, and as I drove away their mate was making them do just that.

I rang my Swearing Burke friend and told her my sexiness was transcending lecherous men and I was now attractive to seriously drunk young people who thought they'd find me attractive when they were really, really old!

What a joyous end to a quite disturbing Facetime call with Roman. And perhaps a disturbing chapter overall. Dear Reader, if you are still with me, I must congratulate you on your persistence.

Just like a child, I might have to crawl a bit before I can walk. It's uncomfortable, new and I am very impatient and want to run – without having to experience the discomfort of the learning process.

FFS, I can't fake it till I make it

Without going into a foetal position and an anaphylactic state (my Pammy label for a state of severe overwhelm as a result of being allergic to compliments), I am working on self-love.

Not the fakey-fakey self-love – the 'fake it till you make it' stuff associated with some sickening self-help gurus who focus on the importance of happiness – but the true acceptance and vulnerability to feel a deep inner contentedness with who I am, right now.

In the nineties Louise Hay was a household name in the realm of living your best life and positive thinking. She is still considered by many to be a spiritual guru of healing through self-love. I admit to reading only part of one of her books, and since I was convinced I was broken I don't think I was very open to her 'heal thyself' messages. I also admit to scanning the Table of Contents and flipping to the section called 'Generating Self-Love'. The exercise described was to stand in front of a mirror, look deeply into your own eyes and repeat 'I love you, I love you' over and over again. My blood started to boil in anger. Admittedly, at the time of reading that book I had long been in a depressive state and a mentally dysregulated space. It was a struggle for me to go out in public as I believed I was so revolting that people would want to vomit at the sight of me. Whenever I stood in front of the mirror I was filled with shame and self-loathing. I would grab handfuls of my fat to make sure I was totally disgusted by my image. Witnessing myself in any reflective way was abhorrent because I knew what I was – morbidly obese, unfit, and ashamed of what I'd become.

However, I do owe Louise Hay a big apology. I am aware I have judged her based on my ignorance of her work. Sorry, Louise, maybe one day I will read your work with new eyes.

In earlier years it took all of my strength to try to 'fake it' (my diagnosis of The Smiling Depressive probably kicked in about this time) so that I could pick the children up from their pre-school or school and pretend to everyone that I really was an excellent and competent wife, mother, businesswoman – blah blah blah. If only they knew how much time I spent hiding under my daughter's iron-framed single bed, lying on her favourite rug and eating dry biscuits, just to have enough strength to be the cheery mum I knew I had to be. So I hated Louise Hay for her fucking stupid cult that was earning her millions of dollars from spreading this sort of shallow shit.

My psychiatrist once dared to suggest that reading

something by Louise Hay might be helpful for me regarding my lack of self-worth. My reaction was instant – I pretended to stick my fingers down my throat and vomit on his carpet. My rant about her fakeness, her simplistic ideas and my total disrespect for anything positive about my life even made it into the book he later wrote! Here's a plug – *The Red Chair* by Dr John Webber.

Right now, I am metaphorically sitting in my very own roller-coaster of mental health but on a siding. It feels like I am at peace, that I am taking a welcome rest from my ride. I don't have thoughts rushing through my head as I mentally prepare for all of the things I feel I have to do; I am not writing endless lists (did I tell you I sometimes put 'have a wee' on my list just so I can tick something off?); and I am delighted to announce that 'I am in a good place.' This is quite an amazing statement for me.

I finally feel a deep sense of
connectedness to myself, and
I know that I am not broken.

I am NOT broken.

I AM NOT BROKEN!

Yes, I am screaming it in my head with
a wry grin, because I've been going
around the Universe searching for
answers, and when I finally stopped,
exhausted, battered from self-analysis
and internal war zones, a little voice in
my head whispered, 'You dickhead, you
were never broken in the first place.'

FFS, there's no such thing as a Mental Health Spa?

Have I lulled you into a false sense of security yet? Because it's time to get real. Life with depression and recovery from depression isn't easy and the road is ... well, it's a roller-coaster. I've twice been admitted to a psychiatric hospital. This chapter describes the time with the happy ending. The other one, my nightmare in Madrid, is saved for the next chapter.

In early 2017 my psychiatrist suggested I be admitted into the Melbourne Clinic. He'd made these suggestions in years previous as he'd been worried about my mental health and wellbeing for a while. His final suggestion happened on the Thursday before a huge charity event I was organising, and I thought it would be easier to be admitted on Sunday after it was all over. Of course, this was against my psychiatrist's advice. Hmmmmm. When I write that down now it does sound a little bit batshit crazy. Let's set the scene, shall we?

For about three months prior to my admission, I felt like I was spending each day waiting for the day to end, afraid that if I stopped being busy the world would swallow me up. I was having what is referred to as a depressive episode, but I didn't want to admit that I was back in the same old place yet again. It didn't help that when I reached out to a friend, she said, 'But you are a great coach. Why can't you just coach yourself out of it?' The same person had said in the past, 'I find your depression draining. Why can't we talk about happy things instead?' Not at all helpful!

Just a little aside: when I'm in a dysregulated mental state, my mind can spiral more out of control when someone offers unhelpful suggestions. ('Dysregulated' is a new PC adjective currently being used in mental health circles. It's used in preference to labelling people as having dysfunctional, defective or abnormal thoughts. Oooh! FFS, dysregulated is the new batshit crazy.)

Back to the Melbourne Clinic story. In some ways I wanted to have a rest and be looked after, but I was terrified about being in the place where crazy people went. Not only that, I felt totally responsible for the success of the charity fundraising event I was organising and was fixated on raising enough money.

The entire event, from set-up to pack-up, seemed an uphill struggle. I was dependent on my friendship group to support me but hadn't factored in that they might have Pammy Fatigue (a disease common with friends who have helped me in the past and know the exhaustion that comes with that). One of the two friends who had stayed to help me into the dark hours vowed and declared she was never going to do this again.

On the day of the charity event I alternated between being on a super high and hiding in a locked office because I couldn't stand another second of being nice. The super high included walking the streets of the local shopping centre, accosting people while waving around beautiful second-hand clothes that were examples of the wonderful merchandise available at the venue. This also resulted in me being kicked out of the shopping centre for spruiking without a permit. Oops. In the end I think it would have been so much easier to cancel and just donate the money we raised ($1000). I would also have avoided escalating a decline in my mental health and wellbeing.

Once the event was over, I entered the Melbourne Clinic on my own. I tried to make light of the induction process and remember asking, 'Can I be admitted into the Melbourne Health Spa?' I was told in no uncertain terms that I was not at a health spa but being admitted into an Intensive Psychiatric Hospital, and there were no spas available in any rooms. This was my first reality check that I was not in Kansas anymore, and I finally accepted I was being admitted to an institution and had no choice but to surrender to the process.

I was admitted into the geriatric section of the hospital as I was fifty-seven. For the first time I really felt old and vulnerable. My allocated room had a bed, a cupboard with no doors, and a bathroom – again with no doors. This, of course, is how suicide prevention rooms are designed. After answering a lot of questions, I was given a few pamphlets and a red admission wristlet that I was to wear for the duration of my stay. I had to hand over all of my medications, including any that were non-prescribed, and then my bags were searched, which increased my vulnerability levels. I was asked if I wanted to eat with the others in the geriatric unit at 5.30pm or in the main eating area anytime between 6pm and 7.30pm. I chose the latter.

When I went to the main dining area for my first evening meal it seemed very organised. I copied what other people did – stood in line and slowly inched towards this enormous buffet of food that looked quite delicious considering it was mass-produced. All sorts of people were catered for – the carnivores, the vegetarians, the vegans, the gluten-free and all of the other frees I could think of. I chose my food and sat down with my book, which I intended to read over the course of the next two weeks.

I noticed a woman rocking backwards and forwards who had a red wristband just like me. I looked around and saw most people had white wristbands. I scanned the room for other red bands and could see only one or two, and these people did not look happy. (Of course they weren't – we were in an intensive care psychiatric hospital.) I immediately panicked. Had I been labelled mentally deficient? Was I so insane that I didn't know I was insane? Did I need to wear a red wristband so others could be warned about me? This was my obsession for the first night in the Melbourne Clinic.

The next day I hid in my suicide-proofed room except for meals. Sitting in that huge hall with a multitude of white-banded (aka normal) people, I tried to hide my red wristband, except at the food counter, where everyone had to show them off. Maybe the staff had to be made aware of those under higher supervision.

When my psychiatrist visited me later in the afternoon I held out my red wristband and said, 'FFS, why did you label me as dangerous? Why didn't you tell me I was so damaged that others needed to be warned about me?'

He seemed a little bemused and then laughed, which enraged me. Apparently my red band indicated that I had an allergy – in my case to amoxicillin, which I'd discovered a few years ago. It had nothing to do with my mental health status.

I did start to wonder if I might win
a prize in the 'Most Complex Mental
Health Diagnosis' Lotto of Life.

FFS, I'm going mad in Madrid

Here's the story of the not-so-happy psychiatric hospital visit.

In 2017 I was on a two-day layover in Spain before I was to join a ten-day tour of Morocco that included a wedding I'd been invited to.

Unfortunately for me, The Perfect Storm of Circumstances was brewing – I got lost, the place I was lost in was the local drug district, my phone battery died, and I was super jetlagged and alone. I was trying to return to the apartment I'd rented, and all my official documents were in said apartment. Instead, I ended up strapped to a bed in the Emergency Department of a psychiatric hospital for fifteen hours, an experience that continues to haunt me, as do the reactions of some of the people I reached out to when I was in despair.

This is what happened:

* I got lost in the back streets of Madrid for hours.

* I had my iPhone, but the battery was running low.

* I had three different maps of how to get to my apartment, in the form of photos taken when people tried to help me find my accommodation.

* I found out that Google Maps does not identify small streets - at least it didn't back then.

* I was tired, frustrated at not being understood, shunned by people when I asked for help and increasingly scared of the area I was in.

* I felt my only option was to ask someone to call the police to help me since my phone was now completely flat. But the Madrid police weren't the helpful type - think militia and you'd be more on the mark.

* The police did not understand English, did not seem to want to help, and did not have mobile phones to assist me in any case.

* As I was staying in an apartment (not a hotel), my key did not have the address of the residence on it, and the name I had for the apartment was not listed in the accommodation register of Madrid.

* The police asked if I had any mental issues. I made the mistake of saying I was on

medication for depression. Who knows, maybe they thought, 'Crazy lost woman, we can't understand her, she is emotional, in a seedy drug area of Madrid AND on medication for depression - she needs medical help.' Their problem was solved.

* The police (unbeknown to me) called an ambulance to take me to hospital.

* I was forced into the ambulance and thought it best not to resist as I was now very scared.

* The men in the ambulance manhandled me as I couldn't understand their requests.

* I became teary and tried really hard to comply.

* I was taken and subsequently admitted, with no other option provided, to the Psychiatric Emergency Department of a hospital.

While there, I was:

* Kept waiting for ages, and told I was to stay sitting in the wheelchair provided.

* Interrogated about my mental history and asked the same questions over and over again.

* Asked for details about the drugs I'd taken. I tried to explain why I was taking anti-depressant medication and that I was fully functional, just lost and tired.

* Treated with suspicion, as the name of my medication was not known to the doctor, and I didn't know the medical name, only the brand name.

* Misled into believing I would be able to 'just have a sleep until morning'.

* Subsequently, under scrutiny, stripped of all of my clothing, searched naked and put into a plastic hospital robe and expected to sleep with no pillow and no sheet.

* Deprived of water, even though I requested it many, many times.

* Watched while urinating by two male attendants and denied toilet paper.

After a while, having been denied water for hours and having my requests ignored, I walked to the nursing station and requested water and that the Australian Embassy be called. I was scared, vulnerable and alone and needed some support, including a translator.

After calmly and non-emotionally requesting that my requests be actioned, I was told there would be serious consequences if I didn't go back to my room. As a result of me politely refusing to go back to my room until I saw someone calling the Australian Embassy (I was fearful for my safety at this time), the following events happened.

* Five male security guards approached and surrounded me.

* They physically forced me into a position of submission and marched me into a room that had a bed with both hand and ankle shackles.

* They seemed to delight in hurting me even though I was compliant.

* I screamed out for someone to help me and begged to be allowed to go back to my room.

* This escalated my pain and they laughed as they hurt me further.

* I was forced onto this bed, shackled at the waist, wrists and ankles. I tried to be compliant as I was fearful of what would happen if I were not.

* When I begged for the restraints to be loosened, since my hand was already tingling from the tightness, they laughed again and one guard slapped his hand over

my mouth and nose so I couldn't talk or breathe.

* I feared for my life when they started to move my bed, but they were just taking me back to the cubicle I was originally in, where I was now left unattended for many hours.

* When the night staff did show up, they mocked my attempts at asking for water in Spanish ('per favour, aqua, per favour') and continued to call me 'the Americana'. They gave me no water and laughed at my attempts to communicate.

* Sometime during the night I was brutally injected with a substance. I was told in English that I was having blood tests, but when I asked what was being injected INTO my arm I was told 'No English!' To this day I don't know what it was although I do have photographic evidence of the bruising.

* Finally, a doctor from Chile, who spoke both English and Spanish, understood I was being subjected to horrible treatment. He contacted Rosie, who contacted the Australian Embassy. I was released about four hours later.

* My release form is not on hospital
  stationery, is not signed by any medical
  practitioner, and contains many
  inaccuracies.

* The doctor's four-page report is in Spanish,
  and he did not prescribe any medication to
  be administered.

On the advice of the Australian Embassy representative and the emergency medical team of my insurance company, I cancelled my trip to Morocco and checked myself into a hotel in a safe area.

I wasn't fine. I couldn't sleep, I kept breaking into inconsolable sobbing and I couldn't stop shaking. By the next morning, I knew I needed medical assistance to sleep. I tried to ring my psychiatrist (he was on call so I thought he would ring me back) and I also asked to see an English-speaking doctor. This doctor came, read the four-page doctor's report (that was in Spanish), reviewed the medication I was currently taking, and said there was no documentation of what was injected into me the night before. His profound diagnosis was that I was suffering from a stress reaction and a lack of sleep. No shit, Sherlock! He gave me something powerful to sleep. However, complex medical chemicals being what they are, it had the opposite effect. I didn't sleep at all for another night.

I became highly anxious, agitated and extremely angry.

And probably very irrational and paranoid. So I did the only thing that seemed sensible at the time – I decided to berate my psychiatrist for not being on-call when I needed him. I wrote page upon page telling him what I had been through, blah blah blah (probably quite stoned from the meds, the experience and the insomnia), berating him, accusing him of not being supportive – blah blah blah. Dear Reader – yes, this is very embarrassing to admit. When I was writing these seven-ish pages, I thought I was being quite witty and profound! And I was very resourceful. I not only got them scanned BUT managed to find a way to fax them to his office. (What is a fax, some might ask?)

When my psychiatrist finally rang, he was not at all impressed by my wit or depth of insight. I had never experienced him like this before. He was direct, firm and told me he was very worried about me.

He would not engage in any chit-chat. It was really important that I understood the danger I was in, and a number of times he told me to repeat his exact words. I had to agree to follow every direction that he was going to give me.

Apparently I was on a dangerous chemical high (his term) from whatever they'd injected into me, plus I'd also received a massive dose of the wrong sleep medication from the Spanish doctor. (I'd had enough brain-space the night before to actually include the name of the medication.) I was told in no uncertain terms that, on this cocktail, I was potentially a danger to myself and to others.

I had to agree to not leave my room for any reason for forty-eight hours.

He would check on me daily, and I was to follow his instructions and agree to fly home if he instructed me to.

I was to contact my travel insurance company and commit to their check-ins every four hours during the day for these forty-eight hours.

I was to cancel my planned ten-day group tour before the Moroccan wedding.

And I could only go to the wedding with his permission.

I was alone. I was frightened. I was desperate for human contact that might connect me to my old life. So I rang a friend or two.

Dear Reader, what would you do if a loved one rang and told you this tale? The more questions I was asked by others, the more absurd the entire set of circumstances sounded. The fact that they were all true and so indescribably traumatic, I couldn't seem to communicate. And how on Earth could anyone truly understand the horror I had been through?

I was left with some sort of hangover, feeling like a big pile of poo. But the tale didn't end there as I had to fight the insurance company and deal with bureaucratic nightmares that would make Donald Trump proud. I continued to feel trapped by the Madrid nightmare and needed intensive therapy – FFS, yet another addition to the already long list of PTSDs I'd experienced in my life.

P.S. I did manage to get to the wedding. It was glorious and colourful. I pretended to be happy but no one could understand what I'd been through.

One of the hardest aspects of my depression is feeling invisible. I do have regular thoughts that, if I disappeared some people might be sad for a while but then everyone would get back to their lives and I would be a happy memory – if that. No, I am not considering taking my life, but right now I really have to fight to feel I am relevant, and that this never-ending fucking struggle on my own is worth it.

FFS, ask the hard questions

Today a very dear friend asked for my assistance. She was about to make a phone call that she didn't feel comfortable making alone, and she knew I would help her if I could. We joked that I'd introduce myself as her consumer advocate and that I'd be the one who asked the hard questions. We ended up kneeing each other under the table when my questions made the other person squirm a bit. When it was over and she was again feeling in control of the situation, we had a good giggle.

I told her that as her consumer advocate there was a fee because there's no such thing as a free lunch. She knows me well and laughed. My kitchen looked a bit like the Crazy Chef from the Muppets had visited and thrown pots everywhere. It wasn't that bad, but I did have to put a few things away and unpack the dishwasher, and I had been procrastinating for the last twenty-four hours. So I asked if she'd help me tidy it up.

While we spent the next thirty minutes doing mundane things, she started to talk about what she had been doing during the week and shared with me how low she'd been feeling. She told me that just a few days ago she'd planned her exit from life. Her plan included stabbing herself with a very big knife, straight into her heart. She said she wanted to feel something.

My first question as we stood in my kitchen, temporarily frozen in place with bits of crockery or cutlery in our hands, was, 'Are you still thinking this? Do you still have a plan to suicide?'

She convinced me she wasn't thinking like that right now and told me she'd already taken the step to reach out to her therapist, having worked out what her possible trigger was. A question jumped out of my mouth before I could stop it. 'Why didn't you call me?'

She gave me a look of *I can't believe you just asked me that* and then we both snorted with belly laughs. Bahahahaha – what a ridiculous question. I never reach out to her when I'm in the DoDaDs (Depths of Doom and Despair). I knew that I could, I knew she would want me to, and I knew that if I did we would end up having some belly laughs through my tears, but I never did.

There we were, in my kitchen, doing mundane things, and we were having a raw, honest, deeply significant conversation in a very matter-of-fact way about suicide, about feeling numb, about the desperation of feeling empty. The gift I mentioned at the end of Part One lets me be honoured with another person's deepest, darkest thoughts and means I could hold a safe place for her to be open and vulnerable about her life.

What a gift lived mental health experiences can be.

I told her I understood what it was like to feel numb and how pain can bring some relief in times of despair. Being a sincere and helpful friend, I asked her if she felt numb now. I suggested that I could easily stomp on her toes if she wanted to feel something – I would only be doing it in the spirit of being helpful! We both belly laughed again.

Oh, the joy of dark humour.

I then spoke about how her method would be way too messy for me as I would probably be one of the people who'd have to clean up her house! We squawked heartily again.

I'd never told her about my previously planned suicide, but I did now. I boasted that at least my method was so much cleaner and way more considerate for those left behind. I shared how I'd hoarded my medications, knowing that if I took them all at once with a really great alcohol binge I could guarantee there'd be no coming back.

We laughed and cried about how very polite my plan was, including the note I intended to put on our closed bedroom door, giving my husband instructions for what to do before he opened the door so the impact on our young children could be minimised. The ultimate People Pleaser Exit.

I asked her if she was harming herself in any way currently. She said she had been drinking more alcohol than usual and I clarified my question. I asked her if she was physically harming herself – 'doing something to the outside of your body, to feel pain?'

She said she wasn't and asked me why I'd asked the question. I then shared with her how, when I felt my most numb, I found solace in self-inflicted pain. This included pinching myself intensely on my inner thighs, and when that wasn't enough, I scratched certain parts that are not readily visible until they bled. I was so desperate to feel something – anything really – except total numbness!

We cried, we hugged, we laughed, we held each other, and it could possibly have been the slowest dishwasher unpacking in the history of the universe. We looked at each other and said, virtually at the same time, 'It's all just fucked.' Again, we cackled like witches at an annual coven event.

My friend had referred to her exit plan. 'Exit' sounds so much nicer than suicide, but as a society I believe we have to call it what it is. If we are worried about someone's mental health status, it is in their best interests if we do not skirt around the topic. Suicide is such a grounding word. It is real, it is raw, it is honest, and using it really shows that you care enough to ask the toughest question.

It's an uncomfortable concept – it might be making you uncomfortable reading about it – but life is messy and, tragically, too many people say, 'We never saw it coming. I wish I had asked more questions. I wish …' If you are worried, find a way to have a conversation or encourage someone else to.

I have just written over 3000 words for this chapter, sharing with you my tale of woe. Woe is me. Poor Pam Pity Party. (Three thousand words is a heap of words, by the way.)

But a funny thing happened towards the end of my rant about the unfairness of recent events in my life. I actually got sick of myself complaining.

FFS, that's one thing too many

~

Five things I had absolutely no control of happened in quick succession – five events over five days. Each one challenged me in some way.

About four weeks ago there was chaos and pandemonium in a meeting. The new president has his own unique leadership style and is unapologetically confrontational. I won't go into the details since they don't matter that much, but he said things that hurt me to the core.

Then more was piled on top of this: a major toothache and no available dental appointments, an aborted holiday and now unnecessary house-sitters due to arrive, and a desperate search for alternative accommodation for myself since I didn't want to disappoint the house-sitters. I was in turmoil trying to put other people's needs in front of my own.

I was on my way to collect takeaways and speaking to a friend hands-free on the phone when my car was side-swiped. I was incredulous and decided I needed to stop the other car, get the number plate and his details. The unfairness of everything that had happened to me over that week blew up my common sense.

I zoomed after him, tooting my horn and flashing my lights. He jammed on his brakes, trying to get me to run into the back of him, which did nothing to calm me down. Then he sped off again with me in pursuit. I caught up with him at a set of lights and he lowered his window.

'What's the matter with you, sweetheart?' he snickered.

In a high-pitched voice I answered, 'You hit my car! You need to pull over and give me your details.'

He mimicked back to me in a somewhat credible impression of my squeaky voice, 'You hit me, sweetheart – you pull over!'

I was beyond thinking rationally. I had no care for my personal safety whatsoever. I was blinded by outrage. I, a very overweight 65-year-old woman, was going to take on this middle-aged arsehole!

Eventually, he did pull over. Some sense of control made me pull up a bit behind him in case he backed into my car – there were no other cars on the road so no witnesses. I also thought to grab my phone. I turned off my car and started to get out to confront him, and as I did so he sped off!

I felt defeated, but at least I now knew the car model and registration. I was so outraged I went straight to the police station. They took the details but I knew it was such a tiny thing for them. They informed me they might not find the driver due to the plates possibly being stolen, but they'd look into it – blah blah blah. Then I remembered the takeaway I needed to pick up.

I found a park but the shop had closed. I saw a light on out the back and I knocked at the window, tears of outrage and frustration pouring down my face. Luckily the young lady came out and gave me my order, and when I told her my tale of being wronged – and also because she probably wanted to get me out of the shop – she gave me a can of soft drink. I went home, ate the cold, soggy food and went to bed feeling quite miserable.

The next day I tried to put in a claim for my car insurance, but because I didn't have the driver's details it looked as if I was going to have to pay $795 excess to get it fixed. When I bleated about how unfair it was, the lovely car insurance assistant told me: 'It's in the fine print.'

Learning about the science and function of the brain has been one of the big aha moments of the past year. There are many functions of the brain and it would be wrong of me to simplify it, so that is exactly what I am going to do. When a mood is highly elevated, the prefrontal cortex (the logical, rational centre of the brain) is the one that goes offline, leaving the limbic system (the emotional centre of the brain) in charge.

When Limbic Pammy is talking, life is very dark and I look at the world through filters of shame and disgust with myself. It takes a special person to listen to me and to know it is not really me.

I cannot tell you how many times I have written limbic texts and emails that have not been positively received by the recipients.

When I'm limbic I'm buried in my emotions, and I've learned the only way for me to access my logical thinking is to become aware of my environment and be mindful of my current circumstances. Questions like 'Where are you right now? What is the day like outside? Are you lying down or sitting up? What did you eat last night?' all make me think logically. They bring me back out of the darkness of my emotional state.

FFS, please insult me, my friend!

This must seem such a strange chapter title – but really, what chapter title has made sense to you so far, Dear Reader? It will all unfold, so please stay with me for the context.

Last week I had some bewildering news about a trusted friend that rocked my soul. When I contacted my friend, I was accused of colluding with a third party and of deliberately sending this person to disrespect my old friend. Like seriously, FFS. I would never deliberately want to disrespect anyone – not even people from my past whom it would be so satisfying to disrespect! You lose so many Angel Points for those sorts of things, it's not worth it.

For two days I was in total shock and doona dived. I didn't understand what had happened.

On the third day – nope, I did not rise from the dead like someone more famous than me – the emotion hit and I knew I desperately needed company. I was delighted and relieved when my son Lazza and his gorgeous girlfriend, Ms Viv, invited me to join them somewhere new for dinner.

On the way to the restaurant, emotional fireworks were going off in my head. All the times I'd felt betrayed, powerless and stupid, combined with all the times I'd felt like a victim, were popping off like perfectly cooked popcorn. Pop, pop and massive explosions of pops. But I knew I had to keep a lid on them. I also needed to stay silent on the fact that this trusted friend was prepared not only to throw out the baby with the bathwater but to toss the whole bath away and burn down the whole fucking house. I know, this is soooo dramatic, but that's how it felt inside my exploding brain. I was on the verge of tears and hoped I could contain my emotions with the distraction of great soba noodles and lovely, light-hearted conversation.

Then my son asked me, 'How are you, Pammy?' He seemed to look deeply into my soul and my lip started to quiver. He asked what was wrong. I wanted to share in a non-emotional way what had happened but the brimming tears wanted to shoot straight out of my eyes like the infamous bazooka tears, which wouldn't have been a good look in a trendy little specialist eatery. So I blurted, 'I just need to go outside to emotionally regulate a bit.'

This was language that Laz knew, as we often spoke about the skills I'd learned in a year-long programme of Dialectic Behavioural Therapy. During this therapy I'd discovered that when emotions were about to become overwhelming there were ways to tame the beasts.

I was so full of emotions that just being outside wasn't enough. I did some controlled breathing while pacing up and down the footpath. That didn't work. I tried dragging my senses back into gear by progressively finding and naming the things I could see, hear, smell, touch and taste. That didn't work either. I tried again, combining my controlled breathing and the five senses exercise. It still didn't work and I didn't know what else to do.

I had the thought that I might look like either a druggie trying to get a fix or a person who had got lost in Madrid and ended up in a psychiatric ward. Unless I could find a way to put a temporary lid on these emotions, I knew I'd have to get into my car and drive away to avoid them surfacing in the restaurant with absolutely no context. I was way beyond trying to explain how I was feeling to my son and his partner. I only knew I needed a circuit breaker.

So I sat on a bench and had the inspirational and completely non-rational thought to ring one of my most trusted friends, Lyn of Swearing Burke Fame. Crazily, she answered straight away – this is never a given – with her typical opening phrase to me: 'Pamelalalalala – how the fuck are ya?'

This was perfect.

Immediately I said, 'Can you insult me, please?' This was so out of context for both of us (remember I was emotionally dysregulated – aka fucking craycray – in this moment) and she said, 'No, I am not going to insult you.'

I insisted, 'Please, can you just give me a good insult?' She refused again, but I desperately wanted to hear something other than the massive explosion of self-hatred in my head. So I said, 'Can you just tell me about the most boring tree in your garden?' Again remember, this is all out of context for Lyn, who said, 'I am really worried about you. Please tell me you're okay.'

Her saying that caused me to snap back to reality a bit and I told her I was safe. I explained that I was sitting on a bench, Laz and Viv were in a restaurant a few doors away, and I just needed a good distraction to put some overwhelming emotions back into a box so I could look at them when it was a bit safer. Of course, my lovely friend then asked me what was happening for me, and I said if I could tell her I would not be asking her to insult me FFS.

In true bestie form, she told me that she was not going to insult me, but she was going to tell me about what a fat pig she was. I said, 'Ooooh, that sounds great.' She told me that she was currently watching what she was eating: she had just looked at a lamington and before she knew it, it was down her 'fat gob'!

Of course I laughed and said, 'Tell me more.'

At this moment a young woman walked past. Instead of averting her eyes from my obvious distress, she looked straight into my eyes and gave me a knowing nod. I cannot tell you (which is ironic because I am telling you right now) how profoundly moving this was for me.

I thanked this woman out loud for acknowledging my humanness and then told Lyn about her.

Lyn said, 'Oh, I bet she is starting to run away now – you must seem like a madwoman.'

We laughed again.

Then, in her brilliance Lyn said, 'Oh I've got a good insult for you.'

'Bring it on!'

Lyn said, 'You big sook. It's not enough for you to be crying – you have to do it in public and get everyone to see you, you public-seeking missile.' Of course, we laughed. She said, 'Oh, great, I am really on a roll now,' and blurted out some other insult that we just laughed and laughed about.

By this time my son was out in the street looking for me. I waved that I was okay and thanked Lyn for her great insults. I promised I'd ring her and tell her everything once I was home safely.

The beauty of this story is that I was able to rejoin Laz and Viv and tell them I was okay and there was nothing that could be done tonight. I did, however, relate the story about how I'd rung Lyn Swearing Burke and asked her to insult me.

The gorgeous Ms Viv's eyes nearly popped out. Laz

acknowledged me for being able to put intense emotions back into the box, and I told him I'd open the box the next day when I was at my therapy appointment.

I am so so so proud of myself, and that's a humongous thing for me to say!

The reason I didn't want to write today or for the last two weeks is that I feel like I might be a bit of a disappointment to you, Dear Readers.

A disappointment because at times you may have sensed I'm emerging out of the hard case of the self-imposed cocoon I've spun for myself. You may have even sensed moments of bravery where, just maybe, I could consider becoming a butterfly or even a hairy-legged moth – that would be fun. Instead, I've been on a complete and utter PPPPP. Poor Pathetic Pammy Pity Party. And I have felt totally justified in doing everything possible to stay in this place. I have been feeling miserable, and I want to stay hidden and safe in my own little bubble.

FFS, AM I ANAPHYLACTIC TO ANYTHING POSITIVE IN MY LIFE!!!????

Ohhh – that's in CAPSLOCK, with loads of exclamation marks (oh, how I LOVE exclamation marks!!!) and question marks and I'm using my Pammy-allergic-to-compliments label again. And yes, Dear Reader, it is as dramatic as it looks!

It's bizarre. All things absurd. Not rational and incredibly hard to explain – except to mental health practitioners, it seems. But here I go.

Over the last ten days, amazing things have happened in my life. There have also been moments of deep despair, self-doubt, and some intense self-sabotage that has impacted the way I've functioned on a day-to-day level. *WTF*, I berate myself. *You should be thrilled. On top of the world! Feeling so proud of yourself and what you have achieved.*

Well, there has been some of that excitement and inner joy, which has been wonderful in the moments it lasted. But there

225

have also been nights when I consumed too much alcohol by myself, for no particular reason. Then the next day – feeling so disgusted with myself and quite unwell – I was only able to function at a survival level.

Here is the series of events that might demonstrate the mental health roller-coaster that I – and I am sure many others – live with and that stays hidden from common knowledge. Actually, I hope I'm not the only seriously fucked one on the planet, though writing that makes me feel mean for wanting other people to suffer so I can normalise my mental illness a little. Oh, the conundrum. However, I hope I have piqued your interest enough to read an account of Life According to Pammy.

Thirteen days ago I finally had the courage to enrol myself in a six-month yoga programme for PTSD sufferers, designed to help them with the trauma and recurring negative thought patterns. I made the call, only to learn that the programme I'd chosen after a huge amount of research was booked out with a waitlist. I'm not sure whether instantly bursting into tears is a common response, but that is what happened, along with my emotional explanation that I'd finally built up the courage, I was sixty-four and would never find peace, and more dysregulated explanations of why I thought I needed to be in that course. I cried even more when the receptionist was sooooo kind, promised to put me on the waitlist and guaranteed that,

226

because I had already paid, I would be in the very next course. She was so lovely and seemingly quite comfortable with people crying on the phone. She even asked if she could recommend an alternative treatment for me to consider.

I whimpered, 'Sure,' and asked what she would do if she were in my place right now – as though she was a trusted friend and not a receptionist! My faith in the Universe knows no bounds.

She said there was a Shamanic Crystal Healer at the same clinic who was amazing and I could have an appointment the next day. Again, I said, 'Sure.'

I won't explain here what the process of Shamanic Crystal Healing is and what actually occurred in the session (go to Appendix 1, page 999 if you are interested), but what I will reveal is that I walked out of that session feeling that something had shifted in my energy, and that some parts of my past were healed. I had forgiven and asked for forgiveness, I understood aspects of myself that had been puzzling me for ages, I felt reconnected with my higher self and my spiritual team, and I knew I was safe, loved, whole and complete.

Whaaaaat? Yes, that is exactly how I felt. I felt at peace, and that I was connected and in control of my life. The next two days were delicious. I was centred, productive, happy, and filled with joy and optimism. Until I was not.

On the night before January 26, Australia Day, I purchased

a bottle of wine, thinking I'd have just one drink. I hadn't been drinking much, and I told myself it was an acknowledgement drink. After two glasses a little voice in my head said, 'You've been so good, and tomorrow is a public holiday – you can have another glass.' And then it was so simple to finish the bottle.

I went to bed and – surprise, surprise – couldn't sleep. Not a wink. I'd taken my medication, drunk lots of water, tried reading a book, listened to a podcast and was down to my last resort, which is white noise. I think I went to sleep at 6am but woke again at 8.30am. And guess what! I felt like a big pile of poo. That was the start of the decline – though some might say purchasing the wine was a guaranteed sign that what was to follow would not be pretty.

Australia Day is fraught with controversy. It's also the anniversary of when a babe was born to a non-virgin mother, in a hospital in Wangaratta and not in a manger. My son! Even though he lives about twenty minutes' drive from me, I knew I wouldn't be seeing my son on this, his thirty-second birthday. Somehow a tradition has developed that he spends the day with his partner and friends, often at a music festival or some other public holiday event.

I woke up feeling sick, guilty and conflicted about the whole day ... and alone. My bubble of feeling connected, loved and contented had vanished. Now this is the part of the story that most people don't understand. Nothing dramatic or life altering had occurred. I hadn't had a fight with anyone, I hadn't been disappointed or let down by anyone, I had absolutely no complaints about my life that were any different from the ones I'd accepted the day before. And I had heaps of things I could do if I wanted to.

As I lay there in my bed, my thoughts were racing. I need to get some sleep. That sounds like a plan, roll over. Nope, didn't work. I'll lie here a bit longer to see if that works. Should I put on a podcast to listen to, or maybe some white noise? Oh, I know, I probably just need to take my morning medication. That sounds like a plan – get up, take your meds or else you'll be even worse off.

I got up and took my meds. Then I noticed my bathroom vanity was cluttered and the sink needed a clean. I hadn't swept the toilet or bathroom floor for ages. I hadn't washed them for ages either! I wondered if I should open the door to let the cats out – at least they'd have fun. But it all seemed too hard and I probably needed more sleep, so I went back to bed. (I did let the cats out.)

As I walked back to my bedroom I noticed the shower needed a clean as well, I saw the pile of clean washing in the basket that should have been put away the day before and, oh shit, there was a pile of clothes I needed to wash soon or I'd run out of undies. (Although I do have close to fifteen pairs BTW.)

I got back into bed, even more deflated than when I got up. To sleep or not to sleep – that was the question.

I decided to hold onto the crystal I got from the crystal healing. (Seriously, stop scoffing, I can hear you from here!) It seemed to be the only sensible thing to do to reconnect with the bliss of feeling whole.

But instead it got worse.

I started to write a list in my head of all the things I needed to do. It seemed excessively long. I agonised over where I should start: wash the dirty clothes, put away the clean ones, pay the bills, clean the bathroom and the floors, write an article about the success of my latest charity event (hahaha, how could I write that when I couldn't even wash my undies?), write a chapter for this book – but tell me why the fuck I think I have anything interesting to say anyway? Why was I wasting my time? What if others knew what a fraud I am? What a crock of shit. My children deserved a better mother. No wonder my marriage failed – I am fat, lazy, useless ... AND THEN I started to get really unkind to myself.

It was better to go to sleep and hope that when I woke up more of the day would have gone by. I could stay there while others thought I was happy and having a lovely day. *Shit, I'm pathetic.* I finally fell asleep exhausted and woke up a few hours later to more shame that I'd done absolutely nothing for the day.

In the past this pattern of thinking would spiral into very dark places for many days, sometimes weeks, at worst for months. But being high functioning, I could still see others and be productive, while convincing myself that I could never tell anyone how I really felt because I was so pathetic. Sometimes I'd spend eighteen to twenty hours in bed, punctuated by outbursts of pretend happiness or productivity. Bless my brain and hard-wired thought patterns, I'm sure they think they're protecting me from something potentially dangerous.

However, this time, at about 4pm, when I woke from fitful sleep, I was able to break the circuit.

I first became aware that I was anaphylactic to positivity about six months prior to this latest case of self-flagellation.

Imagine the lack of self-worth so vividly described above, but instead of a day spent in self-loathing, imagine it stretching out into a week – a week of no showering, phone avoidance, and the cancellation of not one but THREE appointments with mental health professionals because I thought I was so far beyond help that they would feel bad that they'd failed in their work! Yep, it was a dark and extreme place to be.

Had anything horrible, negative or demeaning happened to me to cause this response? Of course not. So, what had caused this extreme reaction – the paralysis, total lack of self-care and inability to reach out for help? In the space of a few days, three things had happened:

✻ I was informed that, as a person of inspiration to the community, I'd been nominated for a United Nations Sustainable Development Goal (SDG) Action Challenge Award in the Mobilizer category because of the project I'd created for a disadvantaged village in remote Western Uganda. The project had produced results in fifteen out of the seventeen UN SDGs.

✻ An Australian Rotary magazine had published an article about The Amasiko Partnership - my charity in Uganda - and had included a commendatory letter from the High Commissioner of Uganda to Australia, thanking the partnership for saving the village of 3500 people from Covid despair and reporting on how wonderfully other initiatives had grown. I had shared this article with my large network of supporters and received heaps of positive messages from our charity supporters.

✻ The third, ironically, followed a presentation I did for a Rotary Club on 'Lifting the Lid on Mental Health', in which I spoke about my experience and gave background information and helpful hints on how to communicate with and support friends who might be struggling. I received a number of heartfelt thanks and some people told me how helpful it was and shared parts of their own stories with me.

And that is what led me to more than a week of despair. Imposter syndrome slowly started to overtake my thinking.

The end of the week found me in a chair, in a nightie I'd been in all week. I'd barely eaten, and I'd avoided all communication with anyone when I knew the spiral to the DoDaDs was fast approaching. I finally reached out to my son, who has told me he will always listen. He has great compassion, and once said one of the kindest things anyone has ever said to me: 'Pammy, I will always be your EpiPen!'

So, I sent a text to my EpiPen. I didn't tell him about how tough the week had been for me. I didn't even speak to him on the phone. I just sent him a text to follow up on an earlier Happy Birthday message, asking, 'How are you going, Birthday Boy?' He wrote back saying he and his girlfriend were having a lovely day relaxing and she was cooking him spaghetti carbonara, which he was greatly looking forward to.

My response text asked when we could catch up, and we agreed on dinner the following night. And BOOM, as simply as that, Pammy was back. I got out of the chair, out of my nightie, had a shower, rang a friend, and my new day began.

That event took place about a week ago. Since then

I've been asked to be the guest speaker at an International Women's Luncheon for an audience of about 300, and I have also discovered that a man I met five years ago through a business course has randomly started a business selling tee-shirts and hoodies, all featuring the 'gratitude' theme, and has chosen The Amasiko Partnership as the first charity to allocate his profits to.

It has taken me years of struggle to learn how to break the cycle. And years of acceptance that there will probably always be a struggle, while reinforcing that I have the skills and support I need to break the insidious power of my particular dark spiral. To be dramatic I sometimes call it The Dark Depths of Despair Death Spiral, and sometimes it really does seem that all possible pathways back are that dark. But now I have my EpiPen on high alert to give me a shot or two, and my Swearing Burke Friend to give me a good insult or two if my brain takes me down any Super Fraud Imposter Self-Sabotage Syndrome path, as it is really, really hard to challenge such strongly held beliefs, and the little buggers just keep popping up.

But wait! Of course, there is a clinical name for what I experience during my anaphylactic reaction to compliments. It's well known and so common that 'they' (those who diagnose and label mental health conditions) put a name to it and labelled it a phobia. This is where we all chant – Five Fat Sausages!

The term is cherophobia. *Chero* is from the Greek word meaning to rejoice, and we all know what a phobia is – not a pleasant thing to contemplate. Basically, someone with cherophobia can be afraid when things are good because there might be some rejoicing.

Just when I thought it was safe to come out of the woods – there's yet another fucking disorder to add to my list of diagnoses! And the fact that I find this very funny is testament to my improved mental health score.

My Professional Team Pammy were all amused and amazed at how resourceful I was to find a phobia for wellness!

Deep down I know I'll be back in a cycle of depressed thinking in my personal version of *Groundhog Day*. Unless there is some miraculous, brain-rattling rewiring trick, I'll experience the same thing over and over because my brain chemicals are fucked. I can't seem to find my own self-worth no matter how hard I try, and even with all the therapy in the world there are things I really struggle to accept.

FFS, I CAN do commitment

As a general caveat:

I can 'do' commitment. I get things done. I produce results. Amazing results most times. I can generally be counted on. However, it's extremely rare that these commitments are easily met. To me, a commitment to others is like a sacred oath, whether it's beneficial to me or not, and I'm often left depleted from the effort of making it look easy. There are only one or two people in my entire life who have looked behind the effort and the eventual toll these commitments have on my physical and mental wellbeing.

Did you see how I sneakily snuck in the phrase 'commitment to others'?

Queue in the wailing, self-pitying song – *What About Mee-eeee?*

So ... what about me?

And that, Dear Reader, might be the squillion-dollar question.

Recently I came face to face with this creepy little shitty

amoeba brain of despair – aka Inner Critic. The voice that questions everything I do and gives me reasons to opt out of life – no longer in a suicidal way, but in nearly every other way possible.

All of this synchronises so beautifully with being a single, aging woman locked down in Melbourne (the most locked-down city from Covid in the 'fat' world so far, and we are still racking up days to make sure no other city ever wins this most coveted – NOT – award) while enduring a gruesome, barking, hacking cough. Truth be told I've had this cough off and on for about twelve months. I've had the usual treatments – both medical and herbal – but it's stayed around like that pesky mosquito buzzing in my ear when I'm trying to go to sleep on the first night of my holidays.

So, for something to do I decided it was time to address this cough as it was also playing havoc with my pelvic floor strength. Too much information? Oops – sorry.

This was a positive step forward – good on you, Pammy. Doing something about your health – oh, how very responsible of you! Make some changes! (Insert here other encouraging words.) What I didn't expect from doing the right thing, taking positive steps forward towards better health and wellbeing, was the dramatic and violent ricochet backflip with a twist that I was confronted with.

In the three months of making a commitment to myself

and taking responsibility for my life, the following happened –
in no particular order:

* I got a referral to a respiratory specialist
  to investigate this barking cough that had
  people running away from me in the one
  place I could go - the good old stupid-
  market.

* I had various tests (MRI of brain, chest CAT
  scan, a disgusting breathing test to try to
  induce an asthmatic response, a trip to a
  blood specialist, multiple blood tests), and
  topped up on my Covid vaccinations.

* I had a massively infected tooth that I
  initially ignored and which resulted in
  blinding pain.

* I enrolled in a Trauma-Informed Yoga
  programme that was designed to assist
  healing from complex childhood PTSD.

* And I finally agreed (after avoid, avoid,
  avoid) to have a fasting, complete blood
  test that I knew would throw up some
  challenging results.

In all of these situations I had to reveal what was
happening in my life. I chose to be truthful about my lack of
sleep and poor sleep patterns, my lack of any sort of exercise,

239

my over-consumption of alcohol, the huge amounts of anti-depressants I was on and that I generally Felt Like Shit. (This term was not used on any medical form but I suggest it be included as Chronic FLiSt Disorder. Another one to add to my long list!)

The tooth was a pain to fix – I would rather tell you about pap smears than describe what I had to go through. It ended up being better off in the dentist's bowl than in my mouth. Another one bites the dust!

I went to my first session of trauma yoga. It's a bit embarrassing, but no one will be surprised by now that I spent the first session weeping! For no reason that you might think of but because it was so peaceful, so serene, so gentle, so respectful and felt so accepting that I was overcome with the possibility of inner peace and calm. It was the first place I'd been for such a long time where I felt safe. So, I wept with gratitude. Thankfully I was right up the back and might have sobbed out loud only a couple of times, so I'm thinking not many people heard me.

A massive list of blood tests, urine tests, x-rays and lung capacity tests was ordered to try to get to the bottom of my Chronic FLiSt Disorder. There must be something wrong somewhere?

BTW, my third most dreaded procedure of all time – just behind a pap smear and a bra-fitting – was being weighed and having to hear aloud the very large number flashing on the scale. No matter what the lovely male nurse said or how kind his reaction was, I *knew* he felt disgust for me.

I had no active toxo parasites, the cysts in my eye and brain had not grown any larger and there were no new ones – nor did I have any blood disorders or sexually transmitted germs that might have lain dormant from decades ago. While I could believe new parasites were possible, I hadn't been sexually active for so long that I'd probably regrown my hymen. I had been reVirginated. Oops, a bit TMI, Pammy?

After a thorough and intensive series of breath tests – including a sleep study, surprise, surprise – it appeared there was nothing wrong with my lungs, though what could be more disgusting than being told you are 'a mouth breather with mild sleep apnoea'?

Wearing a sleep apnoea nostril mask with a jaw strap pretty much guarantees no change to my STI status any time soon, and I HATE that I am a snorer who has to wear a little piggy nose breathing thing that either dries out your nose or, if the setting is wrong, starts to gurgle and wakes you up because there is condensation in the bloody hose pipe. Another hit to that diminishing sense of self.

So what did all of these tests uncover, anyway? Basically nothing. No major concerns except to my frail sense of self. I already knew I had a little brain aneurysm friend (not so dramatic – it might have been there from birth), but because of the intense coughing the specialists had to check it hadn't grown. Yay, still there – both my brain and the aneurysm, and neither is bigger.

The results I dreaded the most were the ones from the full blood test. I waited nervously outside the doctor's rooms, convinced I had type 2 diabetes, high cholesterol and significant liver damage. And I felt I deserved all of those diagnoses – I had abused my body and I would have to pay the consequences.

When I got the results I was shocked. Everything – and I mean everything – was either normal or just slightly elevated. I started to sob in the chair, and my gorgeous, take-no-prisoners GP smacked me on the leg and said, 'What are you crying about? These are all good! It's not like you have cancer or anything!'

I kept sobbing but not from relief that I had escaped the machine-gun diagnosis I thought I deserved. My GP did what most normal people would do – she proceeded to tell me how lucky I was. She went on to reveal all her medical struggles and major breakthroughs. As she continued to tell me her life, I willed myself back into control so I could escape her inspiring story!

The irony of it all was that the visit to get my results, which was supposed to be a quick, normal fee, cost me an extra

$60! Because she was trying to perk me up by telling me all about her life, I had to pay the extended service fee! Hahaha.

When I got home I fell into a pit of despair. Back into the PPPP – Pathetic Pammy's Pity Party. I couldn't even tell anyone the good news about my results.

It took me a couple of days to work out that I'd been wishing there was something wrong with me. I wanted to receive some sort of serious, or at least semi-serious, diagnosis that might help me hide the fact that I feel so rotten inside so often. I wanted to have someone worry about me and check up on me. Above all, I wanted to feel I could legitimately ask for help.

Now, here is where I circle back to the beginning of this chapter – about commitment. (Phew, what a relief – there is actually some point to this tale of woe.)

I was face to face with the fact that I am sort of healthy. I wasn't going to suffer or die from some nasty disease any time soon. No one was going to be anything but relieved to hear the good news that nothing was seriously wrong. Sort of healthy means I have no great need to change any aspect of my life unless I choose to. But if I choose to move from being totally unfit and grossly overweight to some new and improved version of myself, that would take commitment. The most offensive C-word for me – even over that other horrible one.

I was faced with:

* ✳ What does healthy at my age even look like?
  Feel like?

* ✳ Is it possible for me? (Knowing me, I would
  have to really believe in miracles for it to
  seem possible.)

* ✳ Would feeling healthy mean that I'd
  continue to feel purposeless but wouldn't
  puff as much when rushing across the road
  to avoid being hit by a car?

* ✳ Would it mean I'd just fill in time exercising
  instead of filling in time mindlessly in other
  ways?

* ✳ Would it mean I'd have to do more washing
  because I'd use more clothes?

* ✳ Would it mean I'd have to shower more
  often, touch my body, maybe see my body
  in the mirror?

Living longer – even if a bit healthier – didn't feel like a bonus.

There's no fanfare here. There's no 'I did it and look how great I am now'.

But there are some signs that suggest I may have chosen to walk into the tunnel, aiming for the glimmer of light at the end.

I've continued with the yoga classes. I rebooked to do the programme a second time because I felt I was getting some benefit from deliberately slowing down my thinking and actually doing some of the practices during the week.

I'm aware that prior to starting the yoga course I was constantly on alert – always scanning my environment for signs of danger, signs that I might potentially disappoint, questioning everything I said or did, and I have admitted that living like that was exhausting.

I discussed all of this with my therapists – my psychiatrist started to sing the Hallelujah chorus!

I've started to take my heart on an occasional stroll and it feels good to be in exercise gear and runners, actually walking and not hiding.

When I get on the scales I say, 'Hmmm – well, it is what it is', and I don't want to hurl them across the bathroom. I do, however, gently push them under the bathroom sink so I can't see them for a while.

I took a three-week job as Census Follow-Up Person. That's not the official title, but I got paid nearly $1000 for walking, getting in and out of my car and delivering notices to letterboxes. I literally got paid to exercise! And I didn't have to talk to people who didn't want to fill in the form. I only had to pop a reminder in their letterbox and check a box on a form to say the house/apartment looked lived in or vacant.

I am on the path towards somewhere. I have made the commitment to living life – not just surviving it.

See – I told you I could 'do' commitments! Even if it's only tiny, petite fairy steps, it is moving forward.

Perhaps I can keep turning up for myself.
For example, maybe I could go out to buy
a helmet and then possibly, just maybe,
take the fully charged electric bike
sitting in my garage for a tiny pedal
down the very safe lane!

FFS – after all this therapy and all this
money (AND no discount for being a
Frequent Flyer or Life Member)
I am back here again.

FFS, procrastination sucks (and it's also expensive)

Okay, Pam. You need to prepare. You need to do your taxes. You do this every year! Every single year you leave it to the last minute; you are so disorganised. Why do you do this to yourself?

You know what to do. Just set aside the entire weekend – this will be your only priority. You have nothing more important than this. And, if you don't do it, you'll have to confess AGAIN to the accountant and she will have to ask AGAIN for an extension, which you will have to pay for, of course.

First up, write yourself a big note for tomorrow! MUST DO YOUR ACCOUNTS THIS WEEKEND. With enthusiastic self-talk you decide you can start tonight, but the panic sets in when you realise you've not kept everything in one place. Some critical and nasty thoughts about how pathetic you are take up quite a bit of time before you tell yourself, *'This is okay. You can do this, Pammy!'* Just write a list of everything you need to gather: the charity bank statement, your Visa, your Amex, your bank statements. You can do this. Just print them all off, AGAIN! Try not to reflect on where the copies of the statements you previously printed are. Then a bright spark flashes in your brain. Why don't you apply a filter to sort through the transactions? Ohhhh, this might work!

Go to sleep on Friday night, knowing that you now have everything you could possibly need printed off upstairs.

Saturday morning: wake up and realise you can't possibly do anything without the right book to enter all this information into. It can't be any book. It has to be the right book. And you need to buy a new one, and you know the right one is green with five columns.

Before you go shopping for the green ledger book, why don't you put on a load of washing? Once the washing is on you might as well wait for it to finish so you can hang it out. While you're waiting, why not unpack the dishwasher, make your bed and sweep the floor?

Next on the agenda, before you purchase a green ledger book, why not look in every single drawer, box and cupboard in the office to see if there's an existing book that you can use? Nope, there are no green ledger books.

Once the chores are done you drive to the newsagent to purchase this book, a book exactly like the one you bought last year. What? They don't have one! They say they can order one and it'll only take a few days. No, you're sure that you can sort everything out this weekend without the proper book.

By the time you return home, it's Saturday mid-afternoon and you're faced with the reality that you've done nothing about anything to do with your tax return. You realise that you haven't eaten breakfast or lunch or had any water to drink. It's time to take care of yourself: make lunch, and eat said lunch with the knowledge that you still need to do your taxes niggling at the back of your mind.

Remain positive. You can do this. You have all the pieces of paper you need – just get an exercise book and you can sort it out.

Start to write into an exercise book all the purchases made for the charity from your Visa, then from your American Express. Feel shocked at how many purchases you've made that you haven't reimbursed yourself for.

Search through your own bank statements. Write down all the payments made to the charity. Try to work out if you've been repaid for these. Realise there's a huge amount of money owed to you. (Avoid! Avoid! Avoid!) Decide that you've worked hard enough trying to do this without the proper green ledger book and you can try to purchase one tomorrow – the right book will have it all make sense.

Eat dinner and settle down to watch something streamed in the lounge. The remote doesn't respond as quickly as you expect it to. How annoying that the button has to be pushed in a certain way before it'll respond!

Go to bed late, having convinced yourself it'll be easy to finish off the taxes tomorrow, knowing you have all of the information you need and you're sure to find a green ledger book at another shop tomorrow.

Wake up late on Sunday morning and decide you need a new television. You've convinced yourself that after last night the other one is totally unsuitable. Just in time you realise you need to refocus, and decide that finding a green ledger book is more important. But before you go out to try to find this stupid fucking book you decide to explore what the ideal TV would be IF you wanted to purchase one. Four hours later, after many rabbit holes of research, comparing different TV specifications and reading so many reviews that making any decision is completely impossible, you end up purchasing a new smart TV that will be delivered the next day. And it only cost $690 instead of $999!

The weekend is over, you have a new TV you didn't really need, the taxes are nowhere near completed and you're left feeling totally incompetent and ashamed of your failed efforts.

FFS! Why would I possibly sabotage myself like this? Again! Why do I inflict this pain on myself each year? All I can think is that when I realised how much money I was owed from the charity, my brain went into a self-deprecating spin. I'd worked so hard for the total amount raised and I didn't want to consider that the money donated by others to reach this incredible result would be diminished because I should pay myself back for my expenditure.

You may have surmised that I don't have a fabulous accounting system, and that avoidance of acknowledging and honouring myself is a teeny tiny flaw of mine. I was aware that I was spending my own money to purchase various bits and pieces, but I hadn't really thought about the impact of that cumulative cost.

I continued the search for the elusive green ledger book on Monday and Tuesday. And now it's Wednesday. I hate the fact I've been totally blindfolded by how to move forward with these accounts. There's no pulling a rabbit out of the hat this time and, finally, I realise I need to ask for help.

Next action, send an email to my gorgeous accountant, tell her the problems I'm having and beg for help. Now, that sounds like a plan!

There are a couple of happy postscripts to this whole 'papers flung across the table, panic, procrastination, pain' event.

I did contact my accountant, who has the hugest heart and laugh. I sent her a grovelling email about how I was having trouble, requested a list, again, of what I needed, asked a few questions and signed it 'from your worst client ever'. She immediately returned my email with all the information

I needed – set out in easy steps – and reassurance that not only was I not her worst client ever but I was one of the most resilient and remarkable women she knew. (I have been honest with her about my apocalyptic views around my financial skills.) That was lovely and gave me the encouragement I needed, and a bit of a system to help my impending-doom brain relax.

Even though my accountant can't understand why a smart woman like me isn't able to update the books every month, do an Excel spreadsheet or organise myself better, she is willing to support me with some persistent compassion. She tells me I don't need the green book, just a spreadsheet. But since she could sense me moving into a foetal position, she said that I could have both – my green ledger book AND a spreadsheet – if it made me feel better. It seems ridiculous as I write this that one can be so impacted by the evil workings of the brain, to the point of not even contemplating giving up the security blanket of a bloody green book.

The other 'Pammy' thing about this whole story is that when the local newsagent ordered a ledger book for me, the only one he could find was a massive red hard-backed thing that cost me $29.95! Apparently they've never made a green, soft-covered, five-column ledger book, so my all-important book was not a thing anyway. After I searched through my filing cabinets to find an old one, it was a green twelve-column ledger book that I had been using all along and I could have easily purchased one the first day I went looking! WTF – once again, attention to actual detail and not some panicky made-up shit would have been useful!

PS: Tidying up my office yesterday while I procrastinated about not wanting to complete this piece, what did I find? Yes – it is true. I found a brand new, green, twelve-column ledger book in the piles of stuff I'd been avoiding for a very long time. Luckily I can chuckle at the absurdity of this whole situation. Will I learn from it? I certainly hope so, but I'm not quite sure yet which part of the lesson will stick in my brain.

What time will you get up today, Pam? How will you get through this day knowing you might not get very many things on this enormous list done? How will you cope when you go to bed knowing that, instead of the list, you've been busy doing other important stuff? Are you just fucking lazy?

I am more and more mindful of why I procrastinate, why I don't answer the phone, why I can't ask for help and why I do the other more debilitating, frustrating and mind-numbing things that I do. But sometimes knowing does not make any difference.

FFS, my girls are big

I tried to explain my healing process to a loving friend (and probably made her even more concerned about me). That when I looked into the mirror it was as if a giraffe was looking back at me – I didn't recognise this new person. Of course, I didn't actually think I was a giraffe (straight into The Melbourne Clinic Happy Home again for me) but my brain was slowly releasing some of my negative thoughts. Even now I can barely think of those non-negative thoughts as positive. How strange is THAT! I'd previously avoided looking in the mirror, especially over the past few years, but now my thoughts were, *Oh, I think I need my top lip waxed* and *Maybe I could get my eyebrows threaded at the same time.*

An even more bizarre thought was, *I am going to have a bra fitting.* WTSeriousF?????

I even went to a fancy bra shop that specialises in everything above a D fitting. (If any men are reading this – presuming anyone at all is reading this – anything above D is a tad supersized. My girls are big.) I joyfully went into the shop, announced that I no longer wanted to wear 'over the shoulder boulder holders' and exposed my breasts. (Relax, Dear Reader. It was in a cubicle with a specialist bra fitting person and my breasts were still encased in some very old and worn-out Kmart Bra Thingy.)

When I finally did expose my girls, my Rubenesque tummy and the scrotum-like sacks I had under my arms were also exposed. My body was being seen in public by two professional bra-fitters and so far, so good. No one had vomited. The gorgeous Zoe even pretended she wasn't scarred for life at seeing so much wobbly flesh. Actually, Zoe was the sweetest and most encouraging person I'd met in a long time. The more outrageous my comments, the more fun bras she found. Who knew there'd be bras that actually fitted and felt good on my bod? I added a couple of sexy bras to the pile and my ADHD exclaimed, 'Why, hello, nips! I can seeeeeee you!'

What really would be a breakthrough would be if someone else saw them, other than one of my besties. (In a particularly ADHD moment, I sent this bestie a selfie of my bright-green right breast in my new bra and she responded straight away with a traumatised emoji and 'What is seen can never be unseen!') Even as I'm writing this, I'm chuckling to myself, saying, *As if.* But the new part of my brain is saying, *Wouldn't it be funny and sort of great if one day, in some strange circumstances, I could be showing off my bra to a potential lover?* Seriously, who is this person? (PS: Can you believe that between the writing and the editing, a lover has actually been exposed to my bras and breasts? And God bless him, he also didn't vomit. Maybe there's life in the old girl yet.)

To venture into the World of Wellness is scary for me because it means leaving life as I've known it and stepping into uncertainty. Apparently I'm not so special, since most others in their recovery periods also find it anything from slightly odd to absolutely terrifying and debilitating. Recovery from acute and chronic major depression had never occurred to me. In my brain it was like having type 1 diabetes – you're on medication to varying degrees all your life, at times it can be very debilitating and there is no recovery. Ever!

I had never really contemplated that I might experience the full range of emotions like other neurotypicals, let alone feel contented and excited without being manic. Despite my life having random moments of happiness, I always 'knew' that depressed thinking would be my constant companion. I am now able to feel at peace much of the day (except when I am extremely anxious because I am feeling peaceful – oh, the irony) and I can deal with emotions that in the past would have plummeted me into deep, intense despair. I do have to push myself, this time not to hide my depressive thinking and dark moods but to accept that positive things can occur in my life without plunging me into a big hole of unworthiness.

In the past my greatest challenge was to make it through twenty-four hours. Now I am waking up with no feelings of impending doom or fear that I will be exposed as a fraud. I am waking up and ready to start the day. But I still wonder: *How can this be true?* and *When will this completely unravel?*

Who is this person who feels alive, who feels good about herself and excited about her future? Who am I without depression and overwhelming negative thoughts and diminishing beliefs?

And she takes a bow – she thinks she deserves one today!

FFS, I CAN do something!

Some of this book was written during the time of Covid, and I must say, I do lockdowns quite well. As a matter of fact, in the last decade I have never been as busy as I was in both big Melbourne lockdowns, because we (our happy little group of sewing volunteers) produced fabulous, reusable, three-layered masks that we sold for the Amasiko charity.

However, I did at times become totally overwhelmed by the collective pain of so many, and the intensity of the massive anti-lockdown protests that Melbourne experienced. And for me, that feeling of total paralysis is overwhelming. There didn't seem to be any reason to get out of bed and I became obsessed with reading everything Covid. It sucks to be an empath – just sayin'.

One morning (well, it was 3pm and I was still in bed) I sat up and said out loud (which is a bit scary when I live on my own), 'FAT FAT FAT SAUSAGES – I can do something. If nothing else, I can be kind!'

I got dressed (maybe even remembered to put on undies)

and drove to the stupid-market. I went straight to the lolly aisle (candy if you are not an Aussie) and bought Fun Packs of all the individually wrapped chocolates on half-price special – Mars bars, Freddos and so on. I had a big shopping bag filled with goodies that I was going to give away. I was so excited.

I drove to the local Covid testing centre, thinking that I could provide a little treat for the testers and the ground staff. To let them know that at least one person appreciated their dedication. Such a good idea!

I waited in my car in a long line to get to the entrance of the testing facility. When I finally reached it I was met by a middle-aged woman who asked me the same question she had obviously asked numerous times: Test or vaccination?

I excitedly told her that I did not need either. I told her I had packets of chocolates to donate so that everyone could have a treat if they wanted. She asked me to repeat myself. When the understanding dawned, her face dropped. She told me they couldn't accept any outside donations, and as a matter of fact they couldn't even bring their own lunches or water bottles. She thanked me quickly and as cars were piling up behind me blocking the busy road, asked me to keep moving. I was shattered.

I had failed in one of the only things I felt that I could do in the lockdown uncertainty I was living in. I momentarily considered slinking away and disappearing into the shadows of my home once again, which would definitely include getting back into my unmade bed. I was thinking, *If I can't be kind, what's the point?*

As I drove slowly down a side road (which I'd named The Loser's Lane because this was the lane you had to take if you were not getting a Covid test or a vaccination), I remembered one of my favourite words. Thwarted. This word and I have a bit of history. I once asked a Landmark seminar leader who had used it in his session what it meant. I didn't have the technology back then to check out random facts before I made a dick of myself, and I asked since it wasn't part of my everyday vocabulary. It is now, and I love using it, but I still cringe about making this poor man feel so uncomfortable – he couldn't really explain what it meant as he had read it out of a manual! Oops. It would have been much kinder of me to go home and look it up in a dictionary but at the time I thought it was such a useless and pretentious word.

Have any of you done a quick Google search on thwarted? I secretly hope so, and I also hope it becomes one of your favourite words too.

So back to the story – I wasn't going to be thwarted. I even yelled in my car as I was coming to the end of Loser's Lane: 'I am resourceful, I can find someone, somewhere that these treats could go to – and not eventually, like the animals on Noah's Ark, two by two into my belly!' If you can eat just one snack-sized treat in a sitting, big kudos to you, my friend.

I was so excited when a light globe turned on in my head. I knew where I could go. I live near a suburb that has one of the lowest socioeconomic communities. I drove to their Community Health Centre, which is notorious for having long wait times and is always very busy.

I was met at the door by a staff member whose job it was to ensure everyone was checking in with the Covid app. I told her that I was hoping the choccies I had might bring a little joy to someone today. She looked in the bag and seemed thrilled. She told me it had been a particularly tough day for all the staff and these would be greatly appreciated. She asked me for my name so someone could thank me officially.

Tears welled up in my eyes as I told her I felt I had to do something kind and was thankful that they might bring a tiny bit of joy to someone. She said, 'That is truly kind of you.'

AND BOOM – I had fulfilled my purpose. I went back to my car and sobbed. I still don't know why I sobbed so much – maybe it was relief, maybe it was knowing I was not powerless and could actually do something kind that might just make a difference to others. Or maybe I am just a sook.

So now, every time I leave the house, which is only a couple of times a week and only within a radius of five kilometres of my home and only for 'legal reasons', I am on a mission to be kind. I am like a kindness-seeking scanner. It brings me great joy to let someone ahead of me at the stupid-market, to make a sincere compliment, to nod acknowledgement or a cheery hello when going for a masked walk.

It feels like I am taking back some sort of control of my life. I am also trying to treat myself with kindness. But that is another story and a huge step forward for the Pamster.

Just like having to sit in the discomfort of negative emotional overload, I also have to sit in the discomfort that life can be positive. And the strangeness of wanting to do things for myself that I have not contemplated for such a long time.

FFS, I'm doing a Michelle!

In 2016, a wonderful role model for intelligence and grace – not only for women but also for humanity – stated, as a response to bullying, 'When they go low, we go high.' This statement by Michelle Obama has become a philosophy that has enabled me to deal powerfully with many adversities, not just bullying. Until recently it was only a great theoretical concept, but now I am putting her theory into practice.

I was recently faced with a number of situations where I felt I needed to channel Michelle's philosophy and take action aligned with 'going high'. Some issues were sooooo exasperating my responses could have gone either way.

One of those situations was a customer service complaint. I had ordered a new stove top that was to be installed with my new benchtops. (I know, this is such a first-world problem – and some of you may be rolling your eyes and thinking, *I wish I had a kitchen – shut up, you pretentious thing.*) Anyway, back to me. When the benchtop people started to install it, they noticed my brand-new stove top was damaged. (A little background to this situation is that, due to a different stuff-up, I'd had no cooking facilities, kitchen sink, hot water or heating for over a week. Oh, poor, poor me.) The installers wanted to finish their job and leave and needed an answer about what to do with the damaged stove top NOW! I stepped into my Pammy Power.

I made a call to the supplier. It was not a great customer experience and didn't in any way assist me with my problem. I have to admit the receptionist was a great gatekeeper, though! She was not going to let any random (my word, not hers) interrupt her salespeople or managers. I needed to understand that it was the end-of-financial-year sale and the managers were all very busy. They would return my call when they could. The call was terminated and it was not by me.

The benchtop men were literally standing with their hands on their hips, waiting for a decision. They were not happy. I was not happy. It was at this point that I realised I had a choice. I could ring back and be assertive. Or I could do a Michelle.

This was the first time I asked the question, 'What would Michelle do?' So instead of ringing straight back, fuming, I decided to do a bit more research about the context of her words. I wanted to do a proper Michelle, not a Pammy's version of what Michelle Obama might do when faced with this situation. It must sound quite ridiculous, Dear Reader!

Anyway, Michelle explained (of course we are now on first-name, BFF status): 'When I want to go low, it is all about my own ego. It's not about solving anything – it is about seeking revenge for the thing that happened to you. Going low is easy, which is why people do it.'

I stood up, stood tall, stood proud (whatever that looks like; it sounds good though) and announced to the world (in my head), 'I am going to do a Michelle!'

I redialled. The same receptionist answered.

I was going to go high. I was going to be understanding, thankful, patient, non-judgmental and seek the best solution I could. I was not going to blame anyone.

The conversation went something like this:

Receptionist – Thank you for calling ... blah, blah blah, it's Erin speaking (made-up name of course).

Me – Hi, Erin. It is Pesky Pam again. I rang ten minutes ago as I just have to speak to someone about a pressing issue that only they can solve. I have tradesmen tapping their toes in the kitchen, and I need to talk to either the gorgeous Di (her real name) or someone else. I am sure that if Di knew about my issue, she would want to speak to me as soon as she could.

Erin: Can you tell me your situation so I can inform you if anyone can address it for you?

Me – Thank you, Erin. (I explained my tale of woe.)

Erin – Di can't help you with that, only a manager can.

Me – Great. Thanks, Erin. Can I speak to a manager, please?

(Michelle – this whole thing is working a charm.)

Erin – Oh, they are all busy because of the EOFY sale right now. (Arrrgh – come on!? I'm doing a Michelle – this shit is supposed to work!)

Me – Erin, when do you think a manager might be able to speak to me?

Erin – I'm not sure – they're really busy.

(Me, starting to scream in my head. Fuck, I have to double down on doing a Michelle!)

Me to Erin – Do you think you could take a note to a manager, and bring it to their attention that an existing customer has an issue and needs urgent assistance? That would be so great if you did that. I'm really in a pickle here. (Would Michelle say pickle? Not quite sure about that one.)

Erin – I'll make sure that as soon as Deb (real name as well) is finished, she calls you before she speaks to another customer.

Me – I greatly appreciate your help, Erin. It must be so crazy there right now. Great for business though, I suppose.

Erin – Yes. (What else was I expecting? That she was going to name her first-born after me? Oops, refocus, Pammy – poor old Erin wants to get off the phone.)

Me – Thank you, Erin. Please make sure you tell Deb that this is time-critical.

Go go go, Michelle! Go go go, me doing a Michelle!

The tradesmen were still tapping their toes. Begrudgingly, they decided to take an early lunch break but stated they had hoped to be finished by now. (Trying to guilt trip me, boys? Haha – that won't work. I have a Michelle in my pocket!)

Fifteen minutes later the phone still hadn't rung.

I stood tall, took a deep breath and channelled Michelle. I rang back.

Erin didn't answer. She must have been on a break or saw my phone number and ran screaming from the building.

I introduced myself to the new receptionist and asked to speak to either the available manager, Deb, or to the salesperson, Di. Amazingly she told me that she was going to put me through. I took a big breath as the call was transferred. The person who answered introduced herself as Deb and said, 'I believe you would like to speak to me?' I announced, 'Houston, we have a problem.' And her response was, 'And I can fix it for you. Let's chat.'

I can't tell you how relieved I was. Erin had passed on my message. She had passed on my issue. I had totally underestimated her and Deb, who worked out a very acceptable solution to my first-world issue. Her attention to detail – asking me to request the tradesmen remeasure the space for the new cooktop exactly and giving me a massive discount on a better product (although I had to wait another week to take possession of it) – gave me so much reassurance that I felt honoured and was totally thrilled with the service.

I got the solution I wanted and needed with little issue. However, I still asked, 'What would Michelle do?'

I needed to go higher. I needed to acknowledge how great the service was, even though it had been a potentially difficult situation, and to ensure that others knew about it.

I did some research on the company, and I found an email address for the CEO.

I wrote a rave review of how fabulous the manager and salesperson were in service and post-service. The owner of this very large Australian appliance company rang me to thank me personally for the great feedback.

I shared with him about how I'd been channelling Michelle, giving others the benefit of the doubt, and as a result received outstanding customer service. I encouraged him to create a Customer Service Excellence Award and suggested he call it The Michelle Award.

I may not have matched Michelle's grace and dignity, but I gave it a good Aussie Shot.

I've also been sharing elsewhere how doing a Michelle has kept me grounded and peaceful. So many people I've spoken to love-love-love the concept of doing a Michelle. I'm hopeful that this movement will take on as a trend, and will bring more peace and compassion to others' interactions where previously a relationship has seemed difficult.

273

Michelle, thank you so much for being you. Thank you for your courage, your humanity and your approachability. In another life we might have been best friends. We would probably laugh, cry, hug and create enormous possibilities for both of our lives regularly. Meanwhile, if you ever come to Melbourne, Australia, do get in touch.

With great highs come the possibility of great lows. Sometimes it occurs to me that I'm stuck in the never-ending loops without realising I can get off the bloody ride.

FFS, how can I be getting worse when I am getting better?

Oh, the roller-coaster is baaaack! Those of us who experience depression often dream of recovering from living a life in the deepest, darkest doom of despair. We want to stop feeling like we're wading through quicksand, or at least stop waking up and greeting each day with dread because it's another twenty-four hours we have to get through.

We try to hide the desperate sense of unworthiness and sadness, knowing that even moments of joy will be fleeting and soon the lurking hollowness will reappear. But as someone famous once said, 'You can run but you can't hide.' That sense of foreboding is ever-present – until it's not. And then the shit really hits the fan!

Of course, my ADHD brain jumped off on a tangent and I had to look up who that famous someone was. Don't lie, I know some of you have already been scrolling. To save you the trouble, this saying originated in the United States in the 1940s and is attributed to the late, great boxing legend Joe

Louis, describing his impending fight with light heavyweight champion Billy Conn. Poor Billy Conn, I feel for him. Joe Louis was famous – both in the ring and out of it – and now has a great saying attached to his legend, whereas I'd never heard of Billy Conn.

And now I've looked up Billy Conn! But I'll leave that little surprise for you to be driven crazy by until you too have to look him up. (Hint – he's very handsome!)

So, yes, I sometimes get worse as I get better. I'm still stepping into the unknown in the belief it will be worth the risk. But now I get to choose the roller-coaster I step willingly into.

Just like the ending for this book, which concludes with the next chapter.

Kathy, here's the last chapter draft. I have
no idea what the fuck you're going to do
with it, but you wanted this story,
so here it is. Work your magic!

FFS, good luck to you, Leo Dale

I don't know yet how the last chapter is going to start, but I will begin with a huge thank you, Dear Reader, for getting to the end, whether you flicked through from the first chapter or whether you read the whole thing. I also want to assure you that, while the roller-coaster ride continues, there have been some massive shifts and I am in the best place I've ever been.

Sometime during the past twelve months I realised I was afraid I'd never feel any pleasant physical sensations again. My emotions hurt so much, but when touched, even by myself, I felt completely disconnected. There have been a few times in my life when I've enjoyed sex, but in the last twenty-five years or so I've just hated my body, and I really wondered if the sexual part of me was dead. I'd lost hope and was instead reflecting on all of the betrayals I'd had. I even started self-harming again because I couldn't feel anything. I was completely disassociated from my body.

Luckily, I realised I was in a bad place, spoke to my psychologist, and started going back to trauma yoga. Around the same time, a gorgeous young male friend of mine told me about all sorts of sexual experiences he was engaged in. It all sounded so naughty and made me realise that I was such an innocent in the sexual realm. But I really trust him, so I told him I was curious to explore whether I was sexually alive or dead. He suggested I might like to come along to a consent party, which involved caring and nurturing touch but not on the sexy bits. Even that felt like too much and I thought if I went I'd probably end up in a foetal position on the floor. But I did tentatively whisper that maybe, just maybe, I could hire someone to help me. I figured if you want the best, you should be prepared to pay for the best.

He said he had contacts (of course he did) and after a couple of weeks gave me a name – Leo. I contacted Leo by email in the first instance. Yes, Dear Reader, I hear your shocked gasp, I actually did it!

It took over a month of emails for me to decide to make an appointment. In that first email I had to be sure I'd told him everything about me so he would be fully prepared. Which meant he had to know that I was divorced, that in my twenty-six years of marriage I'd rarely looked forward to sex and now didn't know if I wanted to be intimate ever again. He replied with far too many emojis (I told him to stop using them but he just couldn't seem to help himself) and made rash promises about satisfying that tingle, exploring with me, delighting with me, and even having me look forward to sex, loving it and loving myself. As if! I immediately replied with many long emails where I disclosed every disgusting part of my background, every self-loathing thought I had and how I was physically unattractive. I was warning him off but, bless him, he wasn't having a bar of it.

I finally booked the first appointment and made a hotel reservation for the night in question. I could get there early, get relaxed, and probably have a bottle of wine before he came.

Inspired by the movie *Good Luck to You, Leo Grande*, in which Nancy, a sixty-something widowed woman, employed the services of an escort to fulfill her sexual bucket list – which included things like oral sex, sexual positions and so on – I created a list of my own.

IN NO PARTICULAR ORDER!!

* I want to receive

* I want to be held

* I want to be powerful in my choices

* I want to feel accepted in my bod and who I authentically am and am not (or have no particular desire to be right now)

* I want to laugh

I WANT TO TICK ALL OF THESE THINGS!!

Before you start getting the idea that this means I was all good to go, let me share some of my messages to Leo over this period.

I actually thought a year ago I would be telling you that you might need a can opener to get access to down there!! Or even a SWOT team of Spiritual Avengers to defend 'That place that should never be touched again'!!

And

I am doing my very best NOT to cancel tonight. Please read the email (haha two emails) I just sent to you so you know how hard I am trying to keep this promise and commitment to meeting you!!!

And

I don't even know what you look like. To me you are just a headless torso!!! So unless you have a sign up with my name on it like at the airport, how will I know it's you from the gaggle of male escorts in the foyer of whatever the name of the hotel I booked??? Do I just stand in the foyer and yell out ... 'Which one of you handsome gifts to humanity is my Leo?'

The day came, I organised my dog and off I went. Having allowed plenty of time to get there (four hours for a twenty-minute drive), I randomly decided to go via the local shopping mall where, equally randomly, I ended up walking into Specsavers and asking if they had any on-the-spot optometry appointments. They did, so I took the appointment, ordered two new fancy pairs of unneeded glasses, paid for them and went back to the car. I still had two hours to kill by this stage so decided to go into the city and get something to eat while I was waiting for the time to tick by.

I started to drive, only to experience a sudden, frightening panic attack. Even with all my mental health issues, I've never experienced anything like it before. I couldn't breathe and I started to sob and shake uncontrollably. I pulled over, got out and walked up and down trying to calm myself. When I still couldn't self-regulate I rang Lyn, my Swearing Burke friend, so she could tell me how fucking ridiculous I was – I really needed someone to make me laugh, and she always delivers.

Having calmed down enough to drive, I headed off again. Ten minutes down the road another panic attack hit. I was shaking and crying and thought I couldn't really, really, really ring her back, could I? But I did. This time she *really* went off at me, which was glorious.

Of course, all that laughter led to me needing a toilet. I finally found one at a pub – yes, Dear Reader, I was tempted to have a drink, but I resisted. I got back into the car and once again the panic attack resumed. This time I decided to listen to a podcast and chose one that was sex-positive. My first ever step into this arena led me to The Good Sex Project. The episode I listened to was about all the different shapes and sizes of the hymen. I hadn't known there was such a vast difference in hymens. This kept me really interested and gave me some fascinating facts I could bring up when I was with Leo, because who doesn't want a good hymen discussion on their first visit with an escort?

I was close to the hotel and by this stage running late. A quick message exchange established that Leo was also going to be a few minutes late. He told me he'd meet me in the foyer, and that he'd be wearing a grey hat and carrying an electric scooter. *How fabulous*, I thought, *I'll know who he is*.

As I pulled up to the hotel I realised with horror that I'd booked one of those really seedy ones in Spencer Street. Anxiously, I tried to convince myself it'd be okay and the rooms would be clean. I drove up the ramp to the car park, stopped at the gate and glanced through a wall of glass into the foyer. A man with a grey hat was already there. He looked like an older European gentleman and had a moustache, which I hadn't known Leo had. I was thinking a bit of false advertising had gone on – this little old wiry fellow was not the sculpted Adonis I'd expected. But he had such wonderful reviews, my friend had recommended him and I'd already paid, so I decided to just go in and meet him.

I parked the car, came out of the elevator and went to the front desk; I didn't go up to the man in the grey hat because I hadn't even checked into my room yet, and it seemed important that I should do that first. Suddenly, the fire alarm went off – a screaming fire alarm, screaming so I couldn't hear myself think, and there he sat with his grey hat on, not moving. I walked outside because the noise was excruciating. I looked in through the front glass. There was no sign of an electric scooter, and I was very relieved to think that maybe it wasn't him.

The fire alarm stopped. I walked back into the hotel only to have the alarm go off again, so back outside I went. I'd pretty much decided the whole thing was too ridiculous when a man with a beautiful bald head that may or may not have been completely tattooed looked at me. He said, 'Pam?' And I said, 'Leo?' He broke into a huge smile and fumbled and tripped over his bag and electric scooter as he tried to walk towards me. We both laughed, it really was comical. Once he finally got himself organised, he opened his arms and I stepped into the most glorious big hug. It might have been my best hug ever.

We checked in but by the time we had the key, my brain was going all over the place because of his warm hand caressing my back. What would everyone think! We headed towards the lift and who should be there but the other man with the grey hat!

'Not this lift! Not this lift!' I hissed to Leo.

The neighbouring lift was filthy, as were the carpet and walls of the corridor we walked down to get to our room. We opened the door and my stomach plummeted – *fuck, I can't believe I'm actually doing this*. Leo asked if he could give me another hug and I stood there in his embrace sobbing from fear, anxiety, relief and overwhelm. I was so nervous and he was so lovely.

I won't go into the specifics of the evening. Suffice to say any innocent touch made me jumpy to the point that a number of times I slapped his hand away – while it was sitting harmlessly on my knee, I might add. I reiterated why I shouldn't be there, going over again all the things I'd mentioned in my emails. I also asked him many times during the evening if it was time for him to go yet. Through all of this he led me with calm kindness, even chanting with me at one point while I was having a panic attack. He tried to follow along with the words but he was doing it so badly and the walls were so thin that I broke into spontaneous laughter, thinking about the couple next door who had a 'do not disturb' sign outside their room. By the end of the evening I was so grateful for this man. He was respectful and I never felt pressured to do anything. All we'd done was hold each other and talk and laugh, but it was the most connected I'd felt in such a long time.

I've been seeing Leo for a few months now – he calls me Pamcy, a cheeky nod to Nancy in *Good Luck to You, Leo Grande*. Each time I see him I feel more free and connected to my body. Sometimes it's very steamy and sometimes we just sit together and talk and laugh like long-time friends.

He never knows who will meet him at the door. And I never know what's going to happen – sometimes I just spend our session sobbing while he listens. He's just a love bubble who I feel a connection with, whether there's anything physical or not. I feel comfortable when I'm naked with him – literally and figuratively. My book coach tells me that being able to be fully naked with someone, emotionally and physically, has to be in the book because it is such a remarkable transition from when she first met me. And now it is.

It's so strange to think there are people who accept me and who believe in me. I've been so overwhelmed by my lack of self-belief when everyone else is believing in me. But you know what I'm doing? I'm showing up. I'm turning up. I'm believing that anything can happen. If I'm panicking, I take a deep breath and say, 'I've got this.' And if one of my peeps is around they'll say, 'You've got this, Pammy.' Anything really is possible. It's unbelievable that some of the people who have read my manuscript have been moved to tears by my stories. And they've laughed too – pelvic-floor-challenging laughs. I'm looking after myself. I'm doing self-care. I'm doing self-regulation. I'm honouring myself. And now, instead of terrified, I'm sort of a little bit excited.

I'm a little bit excited.

Acknowledgements

I am incredibly fortunate to have loving, trusted people who I can text or call when I'm at my lowest and most vulnerable. (I can't name you all here but I will have told you individually that this means you.) These people have all demonstrated that, no matter what I'm experiencing in terms of extreme lows, they are my champions. They listen (even if they have no idea why I'm in such a low) and guide me to confide in and request support from my Professional Team Pammy. They remind me that they actually want me in their lives, no matter what version of me shows up. They accept me as I am and as I am not.

Special thanks to Lyn Swearing Burke, whose dark humour has made me laugh in some of my most dysregulated moments (and who unwittingly provided inspiration for the phrase that would become the title of this book). To my Professional Mental Health Team Pammy – Mel, John, and KC – thank you for believing in me when I couldn't, and for providing unconditional support (plus a gentle smack over the head with a feather when it's been required). Biggest soul hugs to all of my special peeps, Billie, Leela, Anna, Rachel and of course my Leo, who have helped heal my body and soul. Wendy, my long-time friend, thank you for forty wonderful years of friendship and for being gutsy enough to be my first reader and providing valuable insights that have made a difference to this book.

Even though she didn't expect this, I must acknowledge my book coach Kathy Derrick, who is one of the key reasons I've finished this book. Her unwavering belief has always been that I have an important story to share. As an extra bonus, she's become a wonderful friend over this journey together. (And even though I have just met you, I love you, Jac.) Thanks also to my Team DYS who have seen greatness within me that I can't always see in myself. Without them holding space for me, I would not have had the courage to step boldly onto stage for the very first time.

My deepest thanks and love to my children, Rosie and Larry. The privilege of being your mum has taken me on a journey of delight and self-discovery. For that I will always be most grateful.

AND ...

I want to acknowledge myself – I am PAM just as I am.

Pamela Joy Wood lives in a suburb of Naarm in Melbourne, on the land of the Wurundjeri Woi-wurrung people. She has two adult children and currently lives with her dog, BokkiBoi, and Poppy and Clarence, her dog-tolerant cats.

Depending on who she is with (or which country she is in), she has many names. Most commonly she is called Pam, although many call her Pammy. Some call her Pam Bam, PamPam, Pamella and occasionally Pamm-a-lam-a-lam-a-la. And some just shake their heads and call her OTT Pam or TMI Pammy.

In Uganda, depending where she is in the Tooro Kingdom, she is called Natukunda or Akiiki (both honouring names). And when introduced formally there, she is Natukunda Akiiki Pamella.

She used to think that she could be anything you wanted her to be. But she's not willing to do that anymore. She has come to understand that 'I am Pam, just as I am.'

In October 2024 Pam made her artistic debut on stage and presented five shows at the Melbourne Fringe Festival. She performed an hour-long solo show called *Dys-Order-Ed,* which is about reclaiming her life. Her voice matters and it may spur others to find theirs too.

Yep – The Pammy is reclaiming her voice in a major way.

Where to find help in Australia

These are telephone and online support services for people affected by mental health issues. No matter your concern, these are a good place to start. Please send Pam an email if you're in another country and she'd be honoured to assist you to find the resources you need. fivefatsausages888@gmail.com

ALWAYS CALL 000 in an **emergency** in Australia. Or learn your own country's Emergency Responder Number!

A GREAT PLACE TO START for an overview of all available services can be found at www.mentalhealthcommission.gov.au/find-support

For quick reference, here are the contact details for someone in Australia to call in a crisis:

Beyond Blue	1300 224 636	24/7	www.beyondblue.org.au
SANE (free digital and telehealth support for complex mental health needs)	1800 737 732	Monday to Friday 10am to 8pm AEST/AEDT	www.sane.org
Lifeline	Ph 13 11 14 Txt 0477 13 11 14	24/7	www.lifeline.org.au
Suicide Call Back	1300 659 467	24/7	www.suicidecallbackservice.org.au
1800RESPECT (domestic and sexual violence counselling)	1800 737 732	24/7	www.1800respect.org.au
Fullstop Australia (support for people impacted by sexual, domestic and family violence)	1800 385 578	24/7	www.fullstop.org.au/get-help
Parentline Victoria (NB other states have different contact details)	13 22 89	8am to midnight every day	www.betterhealth.vic.gov.au/health/serviceprofiles/parentline-service
Safe Steps (Family Violence Response Centre)	1800 015 188	24/7	www.safesteps.org.au
ARAFMI (carer support line)	1300 554 660	24/7	www.arafmi.com.au/carer-family-support
QLife (LGBTQIA+ peer support and referral)	1800 184 527	3pm to midnight every day	www.qlife.org.au

Pam wishes she could write out every single reference relevant to every single person's needs. (Note from the publisher: She tried!)

Printed in Great Britain
by Amazon

59678036R00172